The Fear Trap

Nick Chapman

Copyright © 2014 Nick Chapman

All rights reserved.

ISBN-13: 978-1505427042
ISBN-10: 1505427045

Foreword

The invitation	11
The beach	15
The magician	23
The sail boat	37
The violinist	47
The sculpture	65
Legend of Osclouro	77
Land of dreams	94
A new acquaintance	112
The fear trap	117
City of Eth	128
A new beginning	134
The secret to success	144

"Recovery starts with curiosity. Take a moment to consider that you may have a gift. A gift you will be able to use freely.

A gift of exceptional energy that will create something amazing and wonderful.

Once you pass through the storm you will find the oasis of peace, this is the true answer to dissolving anxiety and fear.

You will unveil the next level of consciousness and true happiness like hundreds and thousands before you."

Nick Chapman. The Fear Trap.

Nick Chapman

"No problem can be solved from the same level of consciousness that created it."

Albert Einstein.

Nick Chapman

1. Foreword

Please take a deep breath, gently switch off to the sounds around you, make yourself comfortable and start to read slowly.

If you are currently suffering from panic attacks, anxiety or stress, if you are experiencing symptoms that cannot be easily explained, or if you sometimes feel panicky or very upset for no reason, then you are amongst friends. Thank you for reading my short story.

If you are starting to avoid situations for fear of panicking or repeatedly doing something to stop panicking, then again thank you for taking the time to read my story.

I find the most rewarding thing about people who suffer anxiety, panic or stress, is that although sometimes they consciously think they are weak, they are by far the strongest individuals I have come across. I guess you have to be to deal with just a small piece of what gets thrown at you during the suffering stage.

It took me a long while to work this out and accept this, as I felt weak most of the time during my anxious days. When you come out the other side, personal strength is more evident and obvious.

Looking back, it took me a long time to eventually build up the courage to seek help with anxiety or panic attacks. By this time I was at rock bottom, lost in a world of fear, worry, emptiness and confusion.

At that time I had felt places so dark, it really doesn't work trying to put it into words. I kept quiet most of time because I was embarrassed; when I did pluck up the courage to talk to people around me, nobody seemed to understand. It was hopeless.

I had suffered panic attacks since I was just a child. I remember them vividly, at night time, in my bedroom alone, feeling petrified. I remember the severity of the physical symptoms getting worse and worse. I was convinced I was either dying or going insane.

I was terrified and confused; I was so exhausted after these attacks I eventually dropped off to sleep not knowing what was happening to me. Over the years I then went through many years of both anxiety and panic.

I suffered physical symptoms, terrifying and weird mind talk (you may know what I mean). Sometimes there were times where I felt OK and then, when I least expected it or when I just didn't need it, panic would raise its ugly head and do its worse.

I was worried that what was happening to me would just get worse and would never go away. I could not see a way out. The advice and treatment I got didn't help, in fact, most of it made me feel worse.

If you have tried to confine in or explain to somebody "who hasn't been there," then it can be very frustrating for both you.

I solved my anxiety and panic not going through the medical system and not through using talk therapies, but through getting curious about the subject of fear.

I found by shifting my level of consciousness. I could think and feel totally differently. I could face fearful situations, with full acceptance and understanding. I could sit with the sensations of anxiety and then reframe them within seconds.

In a short space of time my symptoms were replaced with a desire to achieve great things. I had a realisation that I wasn't ill, and had never been ill. I was just moving through a journey, like millions of other people.

Of course it was uncomfortable at the time, but it's really nothing to worry about. At the same time you get rid of your panic symptoms and anxiety you will be learning to channel your skills of alertness and energy to develop something amazing for yourself.

You move to the next level of consciousness. You will find a world of peace and tranquillity. A place that is far better than now. Just like everybody who has taken the journey you are about to take.

I recently watched the Disney film Frozen with my two small children. Queen Elsa had the power to create ice through her fingertips. When she finally releases her fear of her innate powers, she turns them into beautiful gifts.

She had two ways to treat her condition. She could try to prevent or get rid of her symptoms or in her words to "let it go!"

By no longer fearing the sensations, you will also turn your energy into a beautiful gift.

I have researched many different methods on overcoming panic attacks and even though there are different approaches, one message is consistent; the symptoms that you are experiencing are basically harmless. Even the worst panic attack with the worst symptoms are usually nothing more than a good workout at your local gym.

I have also experienced people who have suffered many years of anxiety completely change overnight once they shift their level of consciousness and look at the world differently.

One morning as I was boarding a train to Liverpool Street station, London, a story flooded into my head. Within no more than five to ten seconds I had a complete picture of a story about a girl called Ruby and her journey from the depths of anxiety to the higher levels of consciousness.

A story that could give the answers to the reader at both the conscious and unconscious level. I quickly scrawled down on piece of paper thirteen chapter headings. The Fear Trap is the result.

So if I may ask, please un-clench your fists and put your guard down; accept and move on. There is no need to fight any more.

Just sit back and read the words, knowing that the sensations of feeling and thought cannot harm you.

1 THE INVITATION

Ruby knew it was coming, and although the feelings of panic intensified as she slowly peeled back the top of the envelope, she still managed to feel some happiness for her beloved little sister.

The unopened envelope sat on her kitchen worktop for most of the day. Staring at it whilst sipping a strong espresso she considered just ripping it open without thinking, but her fear was too strong.

What is wrong with me? She asked herself the same old question and the same old challenge that she debated on an almost hourly basis for too many years to remember.

This time it was different.

Something from somewhere was giving her a tiny light of energy to try and move forward, to at least just try? 10.30pm was the final agreed time she had negotiated with herself.

Ruby looked up at the clock on the wall, it was 10.15pm and unusually warm for London. The early hot days of summer had provided everybody in England a welcomed lift. The beautiful sounds of birdsong, cricket on the green and joyous beer gardens were all out from hibernation and in full flow.

However, Ruby's fearful thoughts were drowning out these uplifting feelings. The beauty of the world could not be enjoyed at this moment in time.

Ruby grew up in a normal family with her sister in a small town in the north of England. Her parents worked hard to earn money to bring up the family.

Ruby lived a relatively uneventful life, she enjoyed her family holidays and enjoyed sharing times with her friends. Everything was fine until one unforgettable day when she was just fourteen years old.

It happened at night. Ruby had just switched off her bedroom light, lay down in her bed and closed her eyes to sleep, when a sudden surge of what can only be described as extreme terror consumed her body. The intensity of panic that then flowed through every muscle in her body was unbearable. It started with butterflies and cramps in her stomach, and then moved to her heart, which started to beat fast and hard. She could not breathe and her arms started to tingle. Her thoughts were racing, terrible dark thoughts were consuming her mind. She thought she was dying and in that moment she hoped she would, just to stop the suffering. Eventually exhaustion set in and she drifted off to sleep not knowing what had happened to her.

From that night onwards, Ruby suffered from panic attacks and generalised anxiety disorder. She became fearful of her condition and was always on guard waiting for the next panic attack to hit. Her thoughts would convince her that the next attack would be the worst, more than she would be able to cope with.

Ruby's fear trap was born.

On many occasions it did get worse. She was often rushed into Accident and Emergency with a new mix of symptoms suspecting a heart attack. After being wired up to heart monitors and examined by doctors she was sent home with sedation pills and told to rest.

Ruby was embarrassed about her condition and became an expert in finding ways to hide it. She suffered alone most of the time. Her doctor sent her to a therapist, whose techniques seemed to make her feel worse. She tried to talk to her parents, but they didn't understand and tried to change the subject rather than face this dark conversation.

In her teens and twenties, Ruby found a way of coping with the panic attacks by avoiding any situation that was likely to trigger an attack. She avoided going to social events, being in crowded places, dating guys and doing anything she thought would trigger panic. This resulted in numerous periods of depression. Ruby threw herself into her work; the regular routine of her job working in a flower shop acted as a welcomed distraction.

Ruby moved to London in her early thirties and lived life alone in a small rented flat with her pet cat, the love of her life. She was able to cope with her simple existence. She was anxious and still had panic attacks, but they were less frequent and her medication would tend to get her through the bad days.

Now in her early forties, she often had periods of anger and regret about the life she missed out on, and due to a medical problem she was told she could no longer have children. Ruby was angry at the doctors, her parents, her teachers and life in general. Why did this have to happen to her?

The clock struck 10.30p.m.

Ruby finally opened the envelope, the usual symptoms of intense fear flowed through her body, but determination on this occasion won over. She removed the gold lined charcoal card.

Through blurred vision, a shaky hand and chattering mind talk, the following words were read.

My dear Sister,

Maddie Isabel Jones and Mike Dermot Wilson request the honour of your presence at their marriage on Saturday, the seventh of September at St Michael's church, Riverside drive and then at the Belleview Grand Hotel, Surrey.

It followed with a hand written message.

I've always wanted you to be my head bridesmaid. I fully understand that this may be too much for you, and don't want to put any pressure on you coming if you are not up to it. You will always be my wonderful sister! Hey imagine it, your little sister finally getting married – Love you and see you soon - Maddie xxx.

So there it was, a simple day out celebrating her sister's wedding would now become an event to dread. All the worst possible things to fear piled into one day.

There is no way I can go. She will understand. It will be fine. She even said on the card she understands.

As Ruby convinced herself of her decision, the symptoms of anxiety slowly subsided and exhaustion set in. It had been a particularly bad day today; maybe tomorrow would be better? It could not be worse, could it?

As she settled into bed, the pit in her stomach remained with her and also settled in for the night. Ruby was tired, even too tired to worry anymore. As her eyes closed, a tiny light of energy found its way through the darkness.

At the same time her eyelids touched together the tiny light gently rose into her consciousness. With each breath, Ruby sank deeper and deeper into sleep.

2 THE BEACH

Ruby had no idea how she got there, the sand below her feet was soft and warm, and the sun was nestled comfortably in a bright blue sky. The only sounds were gentle waves lapping onto the sloping sands. She inhaled the fresh air and observed her surroundings.

The air had a hint of lemon scent, mixed with lavender. The beach was set in a beautiful cove, a range of mountains provided the backdrop, mature and lazy palm trees were scattered around the sands. The water was clear blue glistening in the sunshine.

In the distance at the end of the beach, there seemed to be a triangular shaped object elevated off the ground. With the sun warming her back, she made her way down the beach towards the object, holding tightly onto her rucksack.

As Ruby got closer, the triangular object turned into a straw roof hanging over a wooden oak circular bar. There was activity going on, she could make out people drinking and gesturing, a low chattering noise travelled through the air.

Around the bar, perched on bar stools sat four characters. What a strange place this was? On the right side of the bar sat a short, but very round creature with a wide straw hat. The creature held a long smoking stick and was inhaling thoughtfully.

Next to him sat a tall lady, with a pointy face and even more pointy ears. She was also inhaling a long smoking stick and sipping a purple bubbly drink from a silver goblet.

On the far side, a large scruffy guy, with a bare-chest wrapped in tattoos, was drinking beer from a huge glass jug and muttering angrily to himself.

To the left sat a smart quiet gentlemen, he seemed very calm and content as he sipped his sparkling water and rested his forearms on the edge of the bar.

In the centre of the bar, an old barman with a large moustache, monocle and a grey cloak was busily cleaning glasses, seemingly unaware of his customers.

The gentlemen to the left slowly moved his head around and caught the eye of the new entrant to the bar. He smiled generously and pointed to the stool next to him.

"Welcome my partner. I've been expecting you," he whispered.

"You wouldn't want to be partnering me sir, I can assure you. Where am I and who are you?" Ruby replied.

The smart man laughed, "My name is Leon and whilst you are with me, it will be better if we are known as partners. Where do you want to be?"

"I don't know, I'm confused" Ruby replied.

"That's ok, don't worry. It will all become clear soon. Fancy a drink?"

"I think I need a strong one" Ruby replied.

The smart man smiled kindly whilst managing to get the bartenders attention.

"Two Red Nails please."

The bartender poured a smooth deep red mixture into two golden goblets and placed them on the oak bar.

"From the great fairy Ena herself, enjoy your drink, relax, sit back and listen. I have a great deal to tell you, your adventure has just begun."

As Ruby sipped the red juice she felt a sudden rush of fearful energy, Leon quickly placed a welcoming hand onto her arm.

"Don't worry, just relax, sit back and listen."

Ruby sat back, the curved back of her stool was cushioned. A reclining leg rest extended from underneath. For a short moment, she felt a rare moment of peace, but the unusual nature of this feeling started to trigger those awful now predictable symptoms, starting with shortness of breath, intense butterflies and chest pains.

Please not now, why now? God help me please. Not here. Where is here?

"It's funny what you ask yourself, when the fear kicks in" whispered Leon.

"Yes" Ruby answered, followed by a pondered thought of "How do you know what I'm thinking."

Leon smiled. "When you've found true magical love and pieced together the ancient teachings of Osclouro, reading people's troubled thoughts becomes one of life's simpler pleasures."

"Reading my mind will not give you much pleasure" Ruby assured her new acquaintance.

"That's where you're wrong my friend. The intensity of those feelings you have, those terrifying sensations, that dark mind talk, that feeling of pending doom. It all reassures me that you are ready to take your journey."

"A Journey? Please I don't want to go anywhere," Ruby said.

"I know you don't, but I am no longer talking to your troubled mind. I am talking to the small energy of light you brought with you from your world." Leon gestured towards the rucksack.

Ruby looked down at her rucksack, which was now swollen and full of numerous moving objects poking out of the sides.

She opened up the top of bag and peered inside. The sight was very difficult to explain. The bag was larger inside, than outside. Objects seemed to be floating in mid-air and there was a mixture of shapes and colours looking uncomfortable.

The more Ruby stared inside the bag the more uncomfortable she got. When it got too much she turned away. Trying to get her breath back, she turned back towards Leon and listened for some explanation.

"Each one of those shapes represents a negative symptom or emotion, they are currently disassociated from your physical body" said Leon as he also peered over.

"How is this possible?" probed Ruby.

"You are now in a world of magic Ruby. Everything is possible. Do not worry about the shapes, you no longer need to worry. Just reach into the bag and retrieve the light"

As Ruby slowly placed her right hand into the bag a loud voice broke the silence making everybody jump.

"More beer!" grunted the tattooed bare-chested man without raising his head.

The light was dome shaped, could fit comfortably in the palm of the hand and contained beautiful colours. Imagine a snow globe full of wonderful mellow light.

Ruby carefully passed the light to Leon, who placed it onto the bar.

"I could have done with this back on that first night of the second moon, when the rain was pounding outside and I received the letter through my post box. I was in a darker place than you Ruby. Filled with depression, anxiety and anger just too hard to put into words. I had no idea who sent the letter it was if the wind had blown hope into my world. The words on the note were written in the ancient language of Eth and were both simple and ambiguous, if that's possible?

It translated like this:

Dear friend,

I must insist you leave your dwelling this evening. If you do, great things are ahead. Meet the magician at 9.03pm in the Old Goblins Tavern. Pack lightly, willingly believe, and stop thinking. When you stop fearing and start loving the world, your world will stop fearing and start loving you."

"There was no name and no address" Leon sighed shook his head and took a sip of his drink.

"So, I was left with a simple choice; stay here in my misery, at least I knew it and would not have to face anything worse. Or pack my bag and find the courage to leave my house?"

Leon continued.

"I read the last line again, when you stop fearing and start loving the world, your world will stop fearing and start loving you. What did that mean? I had tried for years to overcome my anxiety and how can anybody say I did not love things. It seemed to be suggesting that I was somehow doing this to myself. Nobody understood!"

"I looked up at the clock, 8.33pm, I would have to pack, lock up my house and walk to the centre of the village in only half an hour? The last time I ventured to the village it took me over an hour in between the numbness stops, the hyperventilation and constant turning back. I had not left my house since."

"So you couldn't have gone that night?" suggested Ruby.

"Of course normally you would be correct my friend, but there was one thing and one thing only that shook me into action."

"What was that?"

"Curiosity, simple curiosity" whispered Leon.

"Somebody, somewhere was prepared to make an effort with me. Somebody was trying to tell me something. I had to find this magician."

"You did go?" Ruby looked up with growing interest.

Leon smiled and nodded proudly, "and this is where the journey begins my partner relax, stop thinking and listen carefully."

Ruby took another sip from her Goblet, she looked at the label of the bottle behind the bar 'Red Nail from Fairy Ena's famous distillery.' What a weird drink, it seemed to fill her whole body with a mysterious feeling at every sip. She was beginning to realise that there were many weird things in this place. The way out bars back home in London suddenly felt surprisingly normal.

Leon inhaled a short breath through his nose, expanded his belly and then breathed out deeply and slowly, releasing the air from the lower region of his stomach. With each outward breath he made an echoing Ha sound. He repeated this four times.

"May I ask what you're doing" Ruby whispered.

"The breath of fulfilment, taught by the brave monks of Eth" Leon replied.

"That explains it then, silly me!" Ruby shrugged.

Leon and Ruby looked at each other and started to laugh. This first time a light-hearted moment had been shared. Ruby felt pleased with this rare moment of normality.

"I'm sorry, I keep forgetting you're not from this land. We will come back to the ancient monks of Eth later" Leon took one more deep breath and began.

I shut the door behind me; there was no going back. I pushed the long brass key into the lock and turned three times, placed a message to the post elf on top of the letter box and set out down the road.

"It was dark outside, only a few stars had broken through. The cobbled road was dimly lit and many of the dwellings had turned the lights out for the evening.

The rain was tapping a quick step on my umbrella, the wind blew cold into my face, the streetlights flickered and cats danced in the shadows.

With every step my body muscles began to tighten; I focused on moving my feet gradually, one step at a time. I was determined.

I continued my walk down the cobbled streets, avoiding the puddles collecting in the holes in the pavement and trying to keep my rucksack dry. This was tightly strapped to my back and surprisingly light considering the way I had thrown anything in. I arrived at the crossroads in the centre of the village with five minutes to spare.

The high street was to my left, a few shops, the town hall, a motel and a small arched bridge over the river. On the other side was an old red brick building wedged between rows of leaning town houses.

My fear of water was put to one side as I unsteadily walked over the bridge holding tightly to the iron rails. Outside the red brick building was a sign lodged on the trunk of a dead oak tree: The Goblin's Tavern.

Under the rusty sign, a picture of a red faced Goblin sat on a barrel holding his green velvet hat in a welcoming gesture. I could not remember the last time I had walked into a place on my own. I never thought for a minute that I would have been able to do this. Still, I had to put everything behind me for a moment. I had a purpose. I had a magician to meet."

3 THE MAGICIAN

I pushed open the large wooden arch shaped door and entered a darkened heavily beamed room with low ceilings. It was packed with elves, goblins, humans and witches.

The air was thick with smoke and filled with cackling laughter, clanking of glasses and drunken singing. In the far corner a skinny bald man with small round glasses was playing a piano. Two large ladies were leant on the bar wrapped in feather bowers plastered in make-up singing at the top of their voices.

Goblins huddled round small round tables playing board games, witches and warlocks lurked behind in the shadows. The bar was busy. I managed to push through the crowd to order a tankard of ale from the one-eyed bar lady.

I checked my watch 9.02pm. I thought how difficult it would be finding a magician in such a packed place. Just as I tried to work out my next move I noticed some letters of smoke rising over one of small round tables in the corner. It spelt out the words *Magician* and was followed by an arrow pointing down to an old gentleman in a dark cloak and black pointed hat.

I made my way over to the table and coughed into my hand to try and get his attention. The old man dragged over a stool with his foot without raising his head.

I sat down and broke the silence by praising the magician on his smoke trick.

"Blowing cigar smoke through holes in a bar mat impresses you does it?" grunted the magician.

I had no idea how to respond so just cut to the chase. "I was told to meet you here at 9.03pm. My name is Leon, how do you do?"

The magician raised his head slowly. "So Leon, which branch of the higher council are you from?"

"I think you may have the wrong person sir, I was asked to meet the magician through a letter I received half an hour ago" I pushed the letter over the table.

The magician looked down at the letter, hesitated and asked me who sent it to which I just shrugged my shoulders. He then spread a pack of cards face down in front of me and asked me to pick a card.

I reached down picked a card and placed it upright on the table.

"Jack of Clubs, you came alone and have been suffering for some years now" said the magician.

"Yes I have been very ill," I said.

"I didn't say you were ill, I said you had been suffering sir" the magician looked up for the first time. He was younger than I had first thought, maybe in his late fifties. His face was round and friendly.

"I'm sorry, I was not more welcoming when you first sat down. I have to be careful with strangers; hopefully you understand" the magician extended a hand of friendship and we shook hands.

"Why do you say I'm not ill? I have seen many doctors and medicine men and they have all diagnosed an acute anxiety disorder and depression," I said.

"I'm sure they have, and did they recommend the solution?" the Magician asked.

"They recommended medication and therapy for my symptoms," I answered assertively.

"How long have you been in therapy?"

"Over ten years" I replied

"May I look at this medication?" the magician asked.

I placed two bottles of tablets on the table, a strong diazepam to dampen symptoms of panic and anti-depressants to provide chemical balance.

"Interesting, normally I would recommend a slow process of coming off these pills, but on this occasion I really just cannot be bothered."

A flash of light seem to fly out the end of the Magicians finger tips, blue smoke appeared over the table and then nothing.

"Where is my medication," I screamed.

"I'm not quite sure, I have never been sure if they just completely disappear or just move to another location. It is one of those mysteries I have just not been able to resolve. Have you any ideas?" Asked the magician expectantly.

"No I don't care, get them back please!" I shouted.

"Well how can I do that if I don't where they are? Really I thought I just explained that I have never been sure if they......"

"I don't care. I need them" I interrupted.

The Magician looked into my eyes and with a warm smile said, "Like you needed ten years of therapy. You are not ill you are in training. From now on you will be my student, so my advice would be to start acting like one. It will make everything seem a lot easier."

I contemplated a life without my tablets even a day without them; a sudden rush of fear filled my body. Panic filled my mind within seconds, thoughts of doom, insanity, death, a fate worse than death. I visibly shook.

The magician just observed whilst holding his warm smile "The force is strong in you" he joked.

This out of context comment threw me into a short state of relief. Normally, my episodes, caused discomfort in others followed by either strange looks or weak attempts of support.

"How can I control my symptoms without my pills?" I asked desperately.

"You can't" said the magician as he reached under the table.

"Great, thanks for nothing" I replied

"You're very welcome" smiled the Magician.

He continued.

"You see, you don't have any symptoms because you are not ill."

"So explain why my heart is pumping, why I am constantly sick, exhausted, filled with pain and depression all the bloody time" I growled in anger.

"Because you create these sensations. They are not real; they are sensations. In your body and mind they feel very real. I understand that, but they are as real as my last trick"

The magician placed the two bottles back on the table.

"You believed these had disappeared which triggered panic in you my friend. They were under the table. So who created the sensations of panic and were they really real? I'm sure you now feel some relief in your body now these bottles are back on the table, don't you? What if I now said that these bottles are in fact empty and also convinced you that the local chemists were now closed for the week to celebrate the coming of the second moon?"

I looked down at the two bottles on the table, confused.

"What if I told you that the two bottles were in fact exactly the same as you gave them to me three minutes ago? However, I noticed that you had in fact packed the wrong two bottles in your haste twenty four minutes ago back at home, and you now have nail varnish and constipation tablets in your rucksack?"

"Then I'm in trouble," I said

"Maybe my friend, but look on the bright side at least you will have no problem going and your toe nails will look nice! Now, in the same way you chose your sensations, you can now choose to either carry on as you have been or come to the fun side of the island?"

"You seem to know a lot about my issues?" Leon enquired.

"Plenty of time on my hands since I was struck off from the doctors and magicians institute. Bloody unfair in my opinion. All I did was suggest that everybody at the higher council's annual conference were pompous nincompoops."

The magician took a sip from his drink whilst considering his next sentence.

"I mean, the whole point of being in the field of making people well, is to push the boundaries of possibility without any constraints, so when I suggested that the majority of doctors should throw their medication down the toilet and spend more time studying Osclouro's fear trap it caused uproar. Don't get me wrong I believe in medication just not when it's used solely to overcome anxiety. If the institute truly embraced the simplicity of the fear trap then we could change the world"

The magician shook his head and for the first time showed a more human vulnerable side, he continued....

"And everything would have been fine if it wasn't for Bartholomew Archie Case whispering his disgust into the Chief Masters ear during my speech."

"Who is Bartholomew Archie Case?" I asked.

"Bartholomew Archie Case or Barty Farty Face as I call him, is the most pompous of them all, he owns the biggest pharmaceutical company in the land and shared a dormitory with the Chief Master at Lord John's boarding school. He took offence at my comments and pushed his old friend into a decision. So anyway the Chief Master of the institute shut down my practice and struck me off."

"Was there no way you could explain to the master what this Fear Trap taught?"

"It was pointless, the Chief Master had already made his decision, removed my cap from the locker room and barred me from the rest of the conference"

"That is terrible the Chief Master struck you off for just making your speech"

The magician seemed to enjoy my genuine sympathy for a few moments before adding,

"Exactly, Well that and sleeping with his sister on the opening night. Anyway, that's another story and we are short of time. You see it doesn't really matter as I have a supporter on the inside"

"How do you know?" I asked, less sympathetic.

"I receive anonymous messages asking me to meet sufferers across the land and show them the wisdom of Osclouro, just like the one I received an hour ago which brought me to you" smiled the magician.

I took a moment to myself and looked round the room. The scene had not changed; it was as if everybody had claimed their small piece of land and were now desperate to hold onto it. I turned back to the magician who was again reaching under the table.

"What is Osclouro's Fear Trap?" I asked.

The magician hesitated, took another drink from his glass, looked around and encouraged me to come closer.

"Well now you ask, it suggests a small part of you believes there is something out there which will show you how to overcome your condition. Correct?"

I shrugged my shoulders.

"Good. That is all we need at this stage partner. Well done!" The magician gave a friendly slap on my shoulder.

There was something about the magician that made me feel comfortable and hopeful, even though I did not trust or understand him.

"Right now listen carefully………….." the magician whispered, "Osclouro's Fear Trap is simple, very simple. Do you know what a paradox is?"

"I think so, but I'm sure you will enlighten me anyway," I answered.

"A paradox is something that means one thing and at the same time means something else. Once you understand the paradox, and work with both the messages at the same time then you will overcome anxiety forever. The balance in your life will return and great things will happen. It's that simple." The magician raised his eyebrows and nodded slowly.

"So what is this paradox?" I said curiously.

The magician took a deep breath and smiled with intent.

"Let it come in my friend. Your fighting days are over. Lay your sword down on the floor and let the dragon come and get you. Sit back and let it in."

The magician continued.

"Take your shield and place that on the floor next to your sword, you no longer need that either. The more it comes in the better."

The magician placed his welcoming hand back on my shoulder.

"At the same time, build up your power and purpose. Yes, the same creativity that created the energy to give you those unpleasant sensations and thoughts in the first place will be used to create something much more fulfilling and enjoyable. Every human has this built in him or her, without exception. Invite everybody to your party. I mean everybody and then when the time is right start waving some of them goodbye"

"I don't understand, you are telling me to let the awful symptoms come and get me and at the same time telling me to get rid of them?" I asked

The Magician gave a warm smile and placed his hand on his plump belly.

"The answer to a paradox cannot be processed by the conscious mind. This is the key to unlock the fear trap Leon," the magician took another sip of his drink and reached into his bag and placed a playing card face down on the table.

"You see Leon. A paradox cannot be processed in a logical conscious way, which is why so many people fail. Their knowledge of their deeper mind is restricted by their beliefs and boundaries. They are bought into a system that is limited by their own fears. To embrace a paradox you need to stop thinking and trust in your deeper mind to work it out for you, which it will do every single time, without exception. Change happens at the deeper level, not the conscious level."

"So how can I get my deeper mind to help me overcome this suffering?" I asked.

"You just have my friend. By having just a tiny piece of belief, your deeper mind is already starting your recovery. Congratulations!" The magician shook my hand and then pointed to the card on the table."

"Leon, I will be leaving you shortly. You must now follow my instructions. After I leave, turn over this card and then follow the track out of the village staying on the right side of the river. Keep going until you find a little white sail boat moored opposite a small clearing. Take this boat Leon, listen to your doubts, feel the fear and then just do it. Take this boat."

Just as I opened my mouth to ask another question, the magician stopped me and made a nodding movement to tell me there was somebody behind me.

I turned around. The scene had not changed. Everybody was in exactly the same place and there was nobody behind me.

"Very funny" I said, as I turned round to find an empty seat in front of me. The magician had vanished into thin air.

I had so many questions and nobody in front of me to answer them. I was left staring at the playing card on the table. The magician had told me to turn over this card and then to follow the track by the river.

"So what did you do?" asked Ruby. She sat on her stool in silence, completely transfixed on every word Leon had said.

"Well Ruby, I thought I had come this far, so what had I got to lose" Leon said as he took a long drink from his goblet.

He took another two long breaths of fulfilment and continued.

I looked down at the playing card again and without thinking too much just turned it over quickly. I was presented with a picture from the sacred deck. It was the "musician card" and on it written in the ancient language of Eth were the following words "Everybody can sing if they find their song."

Another riddle, I thought, getting used to this unusual night of mystery.

"What's the sacred deck" asked Ruby.

"A series of picture cards passed down through the generations. The legend says that they hold the key to the answers to pure happiness, showing us the path through the symbols and characters," Leon replied.

It was followed by a hand written message. It read; Good luck Leon. You will do just fine. Best wishes the magician.

So that was it. I was left with a set of directions, a sacred card and a riddle.

The Old Goblin's tavern was still in full swing. The piano player had upped the tempo of the music to the delight of the singing ladies and to the disgust of the board playing goblins.

I decided it was time to make a move and made my way to the large oak door. The one eyed barmaid winked at me as I shut the door behind me and found myself once again alone outside in the quiet street.

The rain had stopped, leaving a damp cold feel in the air. Mist was collecting above the river and over the fields ahead. I recalled in my head what the magician has said. Follow the track out of the village staying on the right side of the river. Keep going until you find a little white sail boat moored opposite a small clearing.

I pulled a snack out of my rucksack and looked towards the river. Just below the bridge at the right hand side of the river was a small gravel track leading into the darkness ahead. Well here it goes I whispered, taking a long slow breath. I've come this far. I'm now even more determined to keep going.

The gravelled track hugged the winding riverbank. The moon reflected off the water lighting up the edge of the path. Luckily, it remained bright this time of year. I carried on walking for what seemed miles and miles. I checked my watch it said 11.03 pm. I was getting tired and now worried that this had been a big awful joke.

Was somebody playing with me? The letter, the meeting with the eccentric magician, Osclouro's fear trap, was this just one big terrible joke? Who would do such a thing to me when they know how ill I am?

Just as my mind talk started to accelerate down a very unpleasant path, I heard a gentle lapping noise ahead. I sped up and found myself breaking into a light jog, manoeuvring around the winding river and concentrating on the path. The lapping noise became louder and louder.

I jogged past some tall trees that were purposely reaching out into the river, ahead on the right was a small clearing. I passed the final tree, turned around a sharp bend, and saw a most wonderful sight causing me both panic and excitement. The silhouette of a sailboat moored on the side of the bank.

The magician had been genuine; he did want to help me.

The last time I had been on a boat was when I was a child. The rocking of the boat had made me feel dizzy and sick. We were way out to sea, so I could not get off. This episode triggered a series of panic attacks. I was only seven years old and had suffered ever since. I had developed both a phobia of being on boats and going into water. Up until now, I had managed to avoid both.

In order to board this sailboat I would have to face one of my worst phobias. The thought of this started to cause those awful sensations to boil up inside of me. I immediately reached into my rucksack for my pills.

I pulled out the bottle, unscrewed the top in a panic and poured the contents into my shaking hand. I noticed a small scroll nestled in the pile of pills in the palm of my hand. It read, "Choose to either carry on as you have been or come to the fun side of the island?"

"That bloody magician," I'd like to shove his fear trap somewhere where it hurts. I could not help myself thinking of my own paradox, liking and absolutely hating somebody at the same time.

I tried to recall everything the magician had said, "You create these sensations; they are not real. They are sensations. In your body and mind they feel very real. I understand that, but they are as real as my last trick"

Forty years of suffering a simple trick of the mind. My mind talk started to accelerate again. How can this be something that understanding a simple message will solve? What they don't understand is that I have something much more severe than that. I'm different.

The sailboat knocked steadily against the side, as if it was trying to interrupt my thoughts and get my attention. I tried to focus again on what the magician had said. "Take this boat Leon, listen to your doubts, feel the fear and then just do it. Take this boat."

Well I can certainly feel the fear! He's right about that. Listen to my doubts and just do it? Well that's easier said than done my eccentric friend. My doubts are about everything you said and do it anyway means me boarding the boat and having a massive panic attack causing a heart attack and dying a slow death in a dark clearing on my own.

If I turned back now I would be OK. I could get home put on some hot chocolate, open a bottle of brandy and forget all about this stupid nonsense. I will immediately book an appointment with my therapist in the morning and continue my treatment. That's right; I feel better already. I've decided I will walk back and go home where I belong.

I turned around, jolted my body to adjust my rucksack on my back; breathed in sharply through my nose, nodded and walked back towards the trees. With each step my panic subsided. I feel better already. This is definitely the right decision.

Well done Leon, you have managed to make yourself feel better by taking the path back home. I felt comfortable and hopeful that these dreaded symptoms would leave me alone for the rest of the night.

I felt happy and warm inside, I thought about lighting my wood burner at home, cuddling up with my hot drink and brandy. There was even some chocolate in my pantry I could munch on. I sped up my steps. There was no time to waste. I could be home in less than an hour.

As I walked passed the trees, a small niggling thought entered my head. "I'm sure you now feel some relief in your body now these bottles are back on the table don't you." My legs stopped seemingly against the will of my thoughts. The same feeling of relief I had now was the same feeling of relief I had in the tavern.

He knew I would be in this position when I found the boat; he was preparing me for this. "Let it come in my friend. Your fighting days are over. Lay your sword down on the floor and dance with the dragon."

What did he mean, let it in? Let the dragon kill me off once and for all. Put my sword and shield down and suffer a fate worse than death. The magician was trying to tell me to let the symptoms come into my body. Great advice, I wish I had thought of that forty years ago? Stupid man, now I know why he was struck off.

"You see Leon. A paradox cannot be processed in this logical conscious way, which is why so many people fail. Their knowledge of their deeper mind is restricted by their beliefs and boundaries."

Well right on that one. I have no idea how to process what you're saying you ignoramus. So why am I trying to work this rubbish out then. Why bother if my conscious mind cannot process it. Maybe I should just stop thinking?

"Take this boat Leon, listen to your doubts, feel the fear and just do it. Take this boat."

I looked down and shook my head in defeat. I had to get on this boat. It was my purpose. Turning back and going home was not the answer.

4 THE SAIL BOAT

"I have a phobia of water," Ruby said understandably as she lowered her head.

Ruby had hung onto every single word Leon had spoken. In recent life she had found it very difficult to get in touch with her emotions and normally had a very short attention span when it came to other people's lives.

However, Leon was different. He was suffering the same problems that Ruby was suffering. This somehow, gave a connection, an understanding and a non-pressurised rendezvous that was different from Ruby's normal world.

Leon spoke with a gentle voice, a genuine smile and a non-egotistic confidence. This made Ruby feel a little warmer than her normal cold state, only a little warmer though!

Ruby was still questioning why Leon was telling her all this? Did he just want to tell a total stranger his story to give himself some comfort or was he just proud of himself that he was finding a solution and felt he wanted to share it to make himself feel even better?

"You seem troubled Ruby? What's on your mind?" Leon asked.

"Why are you telling me all this?" Ruby came straight out with it.

"I mean, please don't get me wrong. I'm interested in what happens next in your story, but you see, my life….well you have no idea…. how can I say this……," Ruby started to get distressed; "How can I say this without appearing rude…I'm sorry…I am not really interested in goblins and magic…I have bigger things going on. Just coping with getting out of bed in the morning……I mean my life……..my life is…….."

"Your life is crap. Just plain and simply crap Ruby." Leon stopped Ruby in her tracks with her mouth wide open in astonishment.

"You are depressed and full of fear and panic. You find it hard to enjoy anything. The magic and wonder has gone and you are left with an emotionally empty life; which has more challenges than fun. And anyway what is fun anymore? You have no idea how to associate that feeling do you Ruby. Even if you do get better, is it now too late? Have you got anything left Ruby?!"

Ruby and Leon were both staring forwards, not making eye contact. They sat in silence. Ruby was upset, angry and speechless. Her rucksack was making growling noises and the shapes were pushing aggressively into the sides.

Leon took a deep breath and closed his eyes.

"Ruby. Please listen to me. We are partners. Equal partners. Please trust me as I trust you and if you can't trust at the moment then that's OK. I am not asking you to believe in anything I say. I know how difficult it is coping with fear and anxiety. I have experienced the thoughts. I have felt the feelings. I have suffered the embarrassment, anger and sadness. I have also experienced the emptiness of which words cannot describe." Leon opened his eyes, placed his right hand on top of Ruby's left hand and squeezed it lightly.

He continued, "I'm not even asking you to believe me when I say I'm talking to you because you are on your own journey of recovery right here right now. I am not asking you to believe when I say that you will find hope, love and something magical that will completely turn your miserable world upside down. Ruby, all I'm asking is for you to listen and stop thinking. Even if you don't want to, just pretend for a short while that you are interested and please just listen. Please…will you at least do that for me Ruby?" Leon opened up his hands to invite Ruby into agreement.

Ruby was confused. Why was this stranger so desperately trying to help me? He doesn't know me.

"That was exactly what I thought Ruby, when I received the letter remember?" Leon raised his eyebrows and nodded.

"Reading my mind again Leon?" Ruby noted with a gentle smile.

"That's better Ruby. Even if you don't feel interested or happy, just pretend. In the same way you are questioning whether to carry on sitting here listening to me, I was questioning how I was going to board that boat" Leon closed his eyes again and took four breaths of fulfilment.

"Where did your phobia of water come from Ruby?" Leon asked.

"I don't know. I pretty much fear most things nowadays" Ruby replied.

Leon gave a warm smile, picked up his goblet and invited Ruby to pick up hers. Ruby responded. They clanked their goblets together.

"Cheers" they both whispered. This was now a friendship of understanding.

"Shall I continue Ruby?" Leon asked.

"Please do Leon," Ruby nodded her head and smiled. She was not sure whether something good was going to come out his story, or she was just pretending. It didn't really seem to matter anymore. She was past caring.

"Thank you Ruby," Leon acknowledged.

The scene at the beach bar had changed very little. The bare-chested man was guzzling his beer, and whispering swear words under his breath. The round man with the straw hat and tall lady were lighting more smoking sticks and exchanging the occasional small talk.

The barman sat reading a book on the edge of the bar.

"Are you sitting comfortably" Leon invited Ruby to relax.

"Yes thank you" Ruby responded as she shuffled backwards into her seat.

"OK, so I turned back and walked slowly towards the boat. It was now very chilly and the mist was turning into a blanket of fog. The wind had dropped and it was deathly silent.

When I reached the clearing, I stood a safe distance from the water's edge and stared at the small white boat. Like two gladiators about to go into battle, we stared at each other with neither one ready to make the first move.

How would I overcome my fear and board this boat. I stood frozen to the spot.

Surprisingly, it was the little boat that took the initiative. Two bright blue lamps on the front of the boat flashed on, lighting up the river ahead, followed by a cabin light and a rumble of an inboard engine.

Great, a boat with a mind of its own, inviting me to get on. That's all I need!

I took a few steps forward, now breathing quickly and starting to shake.

The boat sounded its horn and flashed its lamplights impatiently.

That will not help I thought as I unsteadily took two more steps forward. My breathing was so fast I was starting to hyperventilate. My panic was escalating fast and starting to go out of control. I felt awful.

I was roughly five metres from the water's edge. I cannot do this. I just cannot do this. I was frozen to the spot, butterflies were buzzing round my stomach, there was a crunching pain in my chest and my head was spinning.

The Fear Trap

A voice in my head was saying let it in Leon stop fighting. Invite them in. I tried to concentrate on the words. They are just sensations Leon, they are not real. Invite them in and then wave them goodbye.

I took a few more steps. I was accepting the sensations even though they were awful. I had nothing to lose now I was probably losing the fight anyway. My phobia of water was too strong for any solution. I know that, so now let the worst happen to me right here. I shouted, "Come on, come on then." I was out of control.

Feel the fear and just do it. I moved forward again. The boat was right upon me now. I could not breathe; my mind was so fuzzy that I could not think. My stomach and chest felt like they were going to explode.

The boat started to rev its engine, the lamps and cabin light shone brighter. I took one more step and lost my footing.

My body immediately sprung into safety mode, my arms reached out in front of me to break my fall and my muscles tensed to absorb the impact.

I fell into the boat and rolled over onto my back. My symptoms of panic had left me for that split second and I was left trying desperately to get up to disembark the boat.

I held onto a side rail and pulled myself up onto my feet. The boat had moved away from the side, I tried to reach over to the riverbank, but it was no good. The boat had moved too far and was drifting further away from the edge.

I sat back in the boat, exhausted. I reached for some blankets and a pillow that was lying on the rear seat and lay down with the blanket wrapped tightly around me. I thought at least the boat was steady and moving very slowly. The inbound motor hummed quietly. It reminded me of the sound of my mother's vacuum cleaner back in the farm house where I grew up. It gave me some comfort.

This was the last thought I had on this strange day. I was exhausted. I closed my weary eyes and fell fast asleep.

I was awoken by the sound of a small pinkle bird, perched on the flagpole singing beautiful angelic notes. It was a glorious sunny day. The motor had stopped and the boat was now proudly flaunting two large white sails.

I removed the blankets and pulled myself onto the rear seat. I was squinting in the dazzling sunshine. The boat was moving gently up the river. The riverbanks on both sides were full of bright flowers of every possible colour. The air was clean and the gentle breeze refreshing.

I felt calm. I was tired from the exploits of the previous day. I was still petrified of the water, so I did not look over the sides of the boat. I just concentrated on the riverbank and held my body closely to the boat.

The cabin doors opened and I noticed a silver tea urn and basket full of bread rolls. I shuffled my way towards the cabin and ducked under the doorway. Inside the cabin there was a hammock, a small kitchen, clean clothes in a closet and a tiny washroom. I washed, got changed and made myself a hot drink with toasted rolls.

The magician had thought of everything. Where was this boat taking me? I reached inside my rucksack and pulled out the card. Everybody can sing if they find their song. What did this mean? The magician certainly loved his tricks and riddles.

I sat at the table for some time, enjoying the peace and safety of the cabin. The bread was fresh and the elderflower tea was rich and refreshing. I recalled all the events of the previous day, starting with the letter, the walk to the Goblin's Tavern, the magician, Osclouro's fear trap and then falling into the boat. It all seemed like a dream.

The card on the table with the message from the magician was all that I had left to work out my next move. Everybody can sing if they find their song. It was somehow suggesting that I needed to find my song. I presume this was a metaphor for me finding something unique to help me. Where would I find this? I looked closer at the card. There was no map. No obvious clues.

"Ahoy there"; my concentration was broken by a voice calling from outside. I opened the doors of the cabin and stood on the deck of the boat. On the left hand side riverbank three elves were waving their red velvet hats in the air. "Ahoy there, such a beautiful day it is?"

They all had fishing rods, made from tree branches and were grinning from one side of their mouths to the other side.

"Yes beautiful" I replied.

"Where are you sailing on this fine day?" The oldest elf asked.

"Good question, I'm not really sure," I answered with my arms outstretched.

"Well how will you know when you're there?" The elf shouted.

"Good question, I'm not really sure," I answered again.

"Well I hope you find what you're looking for? Good day sir" The elf laughed.

Me too! What am I looking for? The boat drifted past the elves, and carried on up the river. The landscape was beautiful, purple water buffalo were wading through the water, velvet butterflies were floating in the air and the riverbank provided a backdrop of natural colour. Children from the nearby villages were playing in the water, splashing around, laughing and waving at me vigorously as I sailed by.

I felt calm and relaxed, I could not believe I felt like this on a boat, it seemed like that everything I had been afraid of was now slowly dissolving away. I decided to take a peek over the sides at the water.

I made my way to the edge of the boat and peered over. The water was clear with a slight current; there were several small glooble fish following the boat. I started to breathe faster and those same old horrible feelings began to enter my body and mind.

I quickly pulled away, sat down and focused on the riverbank again. Maybe that was a step too far. The sun was now high up in the sky; there were no clouds and just a gentle breeze. I closed my eyes, held my head back and felt a warm feeling across my body. This was certainly a fine day. I was actually proud of myself for the first time I could remember.

The boat moved slowly around a sharp right hand turn. The flowers on the riverbanks were now scarcer and were being replaced by dense bushes with large round red berries. In the distance, I could make out some dazzling lights buzzing around the bushes.

As the boat got closer, the lights became clearer. I could make out body shapes, white flowing dresses, and wings flapping gracefully behind. Each creature was roughly the size of a thumb. There were hundreds of them, buzzing around the bushes collecting juice from the berries in the bushes.

They were beautiful fairies with pretty little faces smiling sweetly as they went about their work. Several fairies landed on the edge of the boat, smiled, waved and then flew off speedily into the bushes. I noticed their tiny hands were covered in red berry juice contrasting against the pure white colour of their dresses.

At the end of the first row of berry bushes, two rather grumpy looking dwarfs were collecting the juice from the fairies into four silver churns sat neatly in the back of a cart being pulled by a donkey wearing a straw hat. A winding track led up to three large timber barns overlooking the fields on the top of the hill. On a sign post, artistically painted in gold swirling letters, were the words "Fairy Ena's distillery."

Several dwarfs were guiding the donkeys back down the hill to fill up more juice into their carts. As the dwarfs noticed my boat floating past, they removed their hats in a pleasant welcoming gesture and then carried on their work without cracking their miserable looking faces.

Wow, even the grumpy characters in this region seem friendly I thought to myself. The little white boat sailed past all the busy activity and out into a wider part of the river. The riverbanks were now being replaced with trees, getting taller and denser as we sailed on.

We continued up the river for several hours, the sun was now lower and starting to break into a wonderful sunset shining through the trees. I had returned to the cabin several times to eat, drink and study the musician card on the table, but was still none the wiser.

We had been sailing up the river all day and I was beginning to wonder if we were ever going to stop. The river was now quiet again; the only life around was the odd bird gliding in the sky and a rare splash caused by a glooble fish leaping out of the water.

The trees were now deep and thick on both sides of the river the light from the sunset was slowly dimming. It was peaceful and felt cooler. I reached for a rather stylish suede jacket that was hanging on a hook on the back of the cabin door and sat on the pillow on the rear seat of the boat hugging a hot cocoa. The sailboat flashed on its lights again, pulled down the sails and started the engine. We motored on into the evening.

I was resting my weary eyes and enjoying the peace and quiet when suddenly the boat decided to sound its horn and flash the cabin lights. I jumped up startled to see the boat veering to the side of the river. It was now dark and I was finding it hard to make out the sides of the riverbank. The boat was defiantly heading for the side but all I could make out was tall dark tree shapes.

The boat sounded the horn again and straightened up against the side of the bank. In between the trees was a cutting, lit up by two candle lanterns hanging from the lower branches of one of the trees. I noticed an old rusty hook lodged in the trunk and threw a rope towards it.

I jumped off the boat, ran towards the hook and tied the rope tightly. I then picked up the rope at the rear and tied it around one of the thick branches to secure it. I collected my rucksack, flask and spare clothes and stood under the lanterns.

The boat had now dimmed its lights, turned off its engine, and was settling in for the night. Ahead through the woods I could see more lanterns hanging. This is the direction I need to go I thought to myself. At least I will be away from the water. I looked back at the boat, and for a very brief moment decided I would miss the little white sailboat that had brought me this far. Liking and hating something at the same time I whispered under my breath.

5 THE VIOLINIST

I walked into the woods, following the direction of the lanterns. I felt unusually calm, it was as if I had used up my full tank of panic and fear and it was sitting on empty. I did not want to dwell on my thoughts for too long in case fear and anxiety returned, so just focused on the task in hand.

I walked from lantern to lantern venturing deeper into the woods. It was pitch dark the only sound I could hear was the crunching of my footsteps on the twigs below. The lanterns were getting more frequent which gave me hope that I was getting closer to something.

Every now and then, a dark worrying thought would enter my mind and I felt my body starting to freeze up. Somehow I managed to slowly move each of my leg muscles allowing me to continue forward. I tried not to dwell on these thoughts for too long, but it was difficult.

The temperature was beginning to drop as the night drew in, I could feel the warmth coming from the lanterns now spaced only three or four metres apart. Up ahead I could make out a string of lanterns leading to a larger light on the ground. As I got closer I could make out a bonfire with some pyramid shaped structures set back around the flames.

The smoke was leading straight up into the star filled sky. I approached the fire with caution. The pyramid shapes turned out to be canvas tents. Next to the fire was a small bench, carved out of one the trees. I could hear music.

I made my way to the tent where the music seemed loudest. The music was beautiful violin strings playing a mellow classical love tune. I stood for a minute outside the opening of the tent. Knocking on the canvas wouldn't work and I couldn't just peer in?

"Hello," I called uncomfortably.

There was no answer. The violin music continued its beautiful tune.

"Hello," I raised my voice.

Still no reply the music continued.

"Hello, Is anybody in there?"

Nothing.

"Hello," I shouted.

"Have you got your ticket?" a male voice with a strong country accent answered over the music.

"What ticket sir?" I replied.

There was no answer again. The violin sounds moved onto a second tune even more beautiful than the first.

"Hello, I am not sure what ticket you are referring to" I tried again.

"The ticket. A rectangle shape" the voice replied from within the tent.

A rectangle shaped ticket. What was he referring to? And anyway why did I need a ticket?

"I apologise. I'm unsure what you mean. I have no ticket sorry. I have come to solve a riddle and wondered if you could help me?" I said politely.

Again, there was no reply, just the soft sounds of the violin. I decided to persevere.

"I was given a riddle from a magician a few days ago, saying everybody could sing if they found their song? You sound like an amazing musician, your violin is wonderful to listen to, do you think you may be able to help me sir?" I asked kindly.

The violin continued, but frustratingly the voice did not utter a word.

"Please sir, I have come a long way and really need some help here. I have no ticket, I would just welcome a few minutes of your time and I will then be on my way," I said in a more desperate voice.

Still nothing. I was getting impatient and felt myself becoming angry.

The music started to speed up and rise in volume. The beautiful tones were starting to be replaced with the odd screeching sound.

"OK, I know I have disturbed you and I apologise, but I am only asking if you can please help me. I have no ticket and don't want to come in anyway. If you cannot help then like I said I will be on my way" I was raising my voice over the music.

I waited and waited. No response. Now I was getting angry.

"I have tried to be polite but it's getting me nowhere. Maybe I should have just barged into your tent, rather than being ignored! …I mean it's not very nice bein….."

"Written down was it?" the voice interrupted.

"Was what written down?" I was pleased and relieved to again hear the voice again.

No reply. The violin music sped up. It was now screeching more and becoming painfully loud.

"Was what written down?" I shouted over the music.

"The riddle, the riddle" the voice shouted over the now deafening noise.

"Yes" I screamed pulling out the card from the inside pocket of my jacket.

As I looked down at the words it clicked into place. The rectangle playing card was the ticket. I quickly pushed it under the flap of the tent.

The violin music immediately stopped. I could hear whispers and the rattling of papers.

The music then broke into a type of celebration tune followed by a joyous Irish jig. A short man with a long ginger beard came hopping out of the tent. He was donning a stripy trilby hat, chequered jacket and playing a small traditional violin.

He was bouncing around, nodding and grinning at me through the whole of the jig without uttering a word. I just stood there looking at him feeling rather embarrassed.

He then finally finished with an over the top finale, like he was performing in a crowded theatre, followed by a very graceful bow.

Unsure what to do I found myself clapping, which sounded very odd in the deathly silence of the woods. The funny little man seemed to enjoy it and slowly raised his body into an upright position displaying his proud smile.

"Thank you, thank you……….. thank you," he waved his arms at an imaginary balcony.

I stood there wondering what I had walked into.

"You hungry?" he said stopping the charade in its tracks.

"I'm ok thanks" I replied confused.

"Good, and me. I will put some food on," he said ignoring my reply.

As he walked away, he left the violin floating in mid-air playing soft classical background music. He wasn't even playing I thought!

He then leapt around pushing pieces of meat and vegetables onto large skewers before balancing them carefully over the flames.

"Drink?" he turned round with a metal mug of cloudy lemonade.

"Urm, thank you" I said accommodatingly.

The funny little man then began arranging two tree stumps and block of wood as makeshift table and chairs. He stood back, rubbed his chin and then rearranged two or three times before he clapped his hands happily. He finished it off by carefully placing a vase of flowers on the block of wood.

"Please sit down Leon," he said as he leant over the flames to turn over the skewers.

I was completely taken back. "How do you know my name?"

"Thought I was a nutcase, didn't you?" The man said.

"No, I just…."

"Yes you did. Yes you did. Don't try and deny it! You will only be denying yourself. Trouble is when you are so absorbed with your own sorry state, you make quick judgements and you're wrong" The strange man was dancing and singing the words whilst pointing at me.

"Well, I can only go on my brief meeting with you, so far you have kept me waiting outside your tent whilst playing increasingly loud music, asking for a ticket you didn't seem to need, pretending to play a violin and dancing round like a three year old wearing that silly hat!"

The strange man stopped and thought for a moment, "Fair point Leon, you're right"

̄ ₁ose the hat, never liked it anyway," the strange man ducked behind a tree and raised his head wearing an even more ridiculous head piece made from woven flower stems and dried fruit.

"That's better," The strange man said tweaking his new hat. He then put the skewers on two metal plates and placed them on the table.

"Take a seat Leon, eat, rest your weary legs, you can sleep tonight in that tent over there."

We sat and talked. I found out his name was Fergus, but he liked to be known as the violinist; he lived alone and spent his days managing the woods as a ranger. He was a happy pleasant guy. He talked in riddles and sang some of his words. He was eccentric but I liked him. All the time we talked the violin complemented our conversation with lovely background music. We talked on late into the night before we both retired to our tents to sleep. I had probed him on the magician's riddle, but he kept changing the subject with more pleasant small talk. I did not push it.

Before I closed my eyes, I was somehow comforted by the chat I'd had with the strange violinist. I was looking forward to seeing him in the morning. I had a long peaceful sleep an unusual occurrence for me.

The floating violin woke me in the morning outside my tent playing an upbeat bouncy number. Fergus was whistling the tune outside whilst packing a bag. He was dressed in a green rangers outfit.

"Morning Fergus"

"Morning Leon, I'm off to check on the deer. Help yourself to tea. I'll be back in half an hour" the violinist replied smiling.

"Oh I almost forgot, think about something whilst I'm gone. Imagine the violin is your emotion; it will play to your tune. You pick the tune, just like a conductor. If you want a happy tune then think happy, if you want a sad tune then think sad. You thought I wasn't playing last night, you thought it was playing on its own. It's just a violin Leon. Beautiful, but still just a violin. Everybody can be a conductor with practice Leon" The violinist disappeared into the woods.

"Just like my bag of shapes" Ruby said pointing down at her rucksack, which was now quiet and still.

"I guess so Ruby" Leon replied.

"How did you think this strange man could help you?" Ruby asked.

"I don't know Ruby. Something was telling me that I somehow knew this man and had just not noticed him. I was trying to think back to my village, but couldn't place him anywhere. It didn't matter though, I had a feeling he had something to help me now."

"I wish somebody had something to help me," Ruby moaned, feeling sorry for herself.

Leon just smiled kindly and continued.

I sat on the bench next to the smouldering fire and thought about what the magician and violinist had said. The violin joined me in silence, seemingly knowing it was time for concentration.

So Osclouro's fear trap was a paradox, inviting and dancing with the sensations and also waving them goodbye. Behaviour changes at the deeper level, everybody can sing if they find their song and everybody can become the conductor of their emotions.

OK, so what did all this mean? The violin played five notes of a small hopeful ditty. Is this violin really playing tunes in line with my emotions? It followed up with four notes of a celebration ditty. Sounds like a resounding yes.

I cleared up the plates and put some coffee on. Then sat with the violin and tried out some emotions; happiness, sadness, anger, guilt. All my thoughts were followed by an accompanying tune. I was careful not to enter feelings of fear, in case I triggered another panic attack, however the more I tried to stop thinking of it the more it threatened to visit me.

I decided to distract myself by clearing up again, but it was no good. Fear was bubbling inside and I could not control it. I suffered a terrible panic attack and this time it was the worst I had experienced for ages. It was most likely due to the fact that something was telling me that my little bit of hope was just that. It was only hope and it didn't really matter what some magician or some strange man was saying. There was no way I was ever going to get out of this. My path was already made, total doom! Why was I deluding myself? It was just making everything worse and reinforcing what I already knew deep down. I was going to suffer and worse still it was going to get worse and worse until it was unbearable? My panic attacks continued to hit me harder and harder. "Why me, god help me!" I screamed. The violin was playing a disturbing out of tune sound and it was dancing around upset in mid-air.

"That's good, good Leon" shouted a voice through the trees. "Find the centre of the storm." I turned around in surprise to find the violinist excitedly running towards me.

"Keep going Leon, keep the fear pouring in. Pass through the centre of the storm. You are nearly there." This odd and unexpected interruption immediately shifted my focus from panic to confusion.

"Keep going Leon, invite it all in, accept the sensations, move towards the swirling energy," it was no good as much as I tried to panic more, my symptoms started to dissolve, until I was left with a body full of nothing and an exhausted mind just wanting to sit and rest.

"Better?" the violinist was unperturbed as he poured himself a cup of coffee.

"You know Leon, those bloody deer. Every time I clear the mess off the pathways, the next morning it's full again!" The violinist was rummaging around in his bags for some food.

"What just happened," I said in astonishment.

"Up to me knees in deer crap, that's what just happened!" the violinist replied distracted.

"No. I mean what happened to me. One minute I was having the world's worse panic attack the next minute it was gone, completely evaporated." I said, still in shock.

"Oh that. Well that's simple Leon. In that particular moment you lost your fear of the fear young man; which meant you could no longer panic, because you had nothing to panic about! Even when you tried to panic, you couldn't."

Fergus took a stick and drew an arrow in the sand. "Here Leon, when your automatic mind senses danger, it triggers a rush of energy. This is called the fight or flight response.

Humans have always had this in their body. We needed it to alert us to the danger of wild animals sneaking up on us.

When we think we can overcome the wild animal with force we release noradrenaline which gives us a boost of energy to go ahead and fight. When we think we can outrun the animal we release adrenaline or epinephrine which prepares our body for flight."

Fergus wrote the words fight and flight by the head of the arrow in the sand.

You see the beating heart, the tension, and those funny feelings. They are nothing more that the body preparing for fight or flight. They are harmless enough, just energy floating around your body.

"The challenge comes now, in modern day, when this primitive automatic nervous system gets a bit trigger happy as it cannot easily distinguish between real threats and illusionary threats caused by our thinking.

So it gets aroused a bit too easily and causes these sensations to trigger when we do not really need them. We get too aroused. You know what I mean Leon," Fergus gave a cheeky wink.

Fergus continued to write in the sand at the other end of the arrow. *Play dead.*

"Then there is acetylcholine, the brake fluid we release when we cool down or play dead. This is when you cannot outrun the beast and you cannot fight because it's too big, so better off sitting down, surrendering and chilling. Maybe the wild animal will just skip around you. This happens a lot when people meet sharks.

I am always amazed how people get so hung up about these levels of arousal, they are nothing more than a harmless release of energy. In fact many sports people will create this in their body on purpose before a race. Heart beating, tense muscles, and eyes popping into blurred vision, butterflies and sickness through excitement. Then the starting gun goes and wow they fly down the track to the finishing line."

"But I cannot stop the sensations when they start Fergus," I interrupted.

"Yes you can Leon, everybody can without fail. You just need to practice. Your body is looking after you; it is just trying to do the right thing for you. So when you get fearful it releases energy for you to fight or flight. Then you think something is wrong as you get fearful of the sensations, so to help with that it releases a bit more energy to help with the fear more. That's why it feels like the panic is getting worse. In reality it is just more energy being released to you, to help you. It's just a trick of the mind and a slight change in thinking completely reverses the process and it starts to dissolve. Accept the fear as just harmless sensations and your body stops trying to help you with more energy.

It ends up doing this after a while anyway.

Through this harmless misunderstood system, people put barriers up in life and retreat from doing all kinds of things, riding on transport, public speaking, speaking from the heart, going out, all kinds of things.

It amazes me, people are focused on trying to overcome or get rid of something that is there to help them. Why would you want to get rid of energy? That same energy that gave you discomfort in the past you can keep and use for something much more exciting and rewarding Leon.

Leon, just practice, don't measure or judge, just practice. Now that you have had one experience of the fear and energy dissolving, your mind picks up the new habit. As you have experienced the sensations so vividly in the past, you will, in fact, become a master of the system and a master of creating energy. More practice and you will be able to control levels of arousal at your leisure from your higher level of consciousness thinking patterns.

This is where your innate wisdom sits Leon. This is where you can focus now.

You are not ill Leon. You are ready to rise to the next level of consciousness, so when you get aroused again, don't fight or run, put your sword down and float through the storm."

For the first time in my life I fully understood. Something was still niggling me though.

"And the long periods of anxiety and depression, where I am just tired and down and cannot be bothered to get out of bed? Where an awful pit sits in my stomach and my thoughts are dark and sad?" I asked.

Fergus smiled and picked up the stick once more. He drew a line horizontally across the centre of the arrow.

"This is where people need to embrace Osclouro's fear trap in all its glory Leon. In our body sit our emotions over which we have complete control. We can be happy and aroused and produce excitement" Fergus drew a sun above the left side of the horizontal line to demonstrate.

"Or we can be negative and aroused and cause high anxiety," Fergus drew a cloud above the right side of the horizontal line. We can also be happy and not aroused and therefore relaxed and content," Fergus drew another sun below the left hand line.

"Or we can be relaxed and negative and feel depressed, tired and detached. This then triggers the fear trap once more. This is a different sensation, but still this illusionary cycle of being scared of the dark thoughts and feelings. This is the same system we all have inside of us. There is nothing to worry about. It just needs a slightly different thought and acceptance of the sensation and then you skip back over to the fun side of the island," Fergus drew the final cloud in the bottom right corner and then skipped back over the sun on the left.

"All it takes is practice" Fergus started jumping backwards and forwards over his picture in the sand.

Fergus stopped and then continued with his explanation.

"The challenge comes when people don't understand the final piece of the jigsaw, which is the crucial piece to putting down the sword.

Our thinking mind does not have much room left when we are sitting on the right side of the line. Especially when we are aroused.

During panic, ninety percent of our body will be taken up managing this, so it only leaves a small amount of room for clear thoughts to come in. That is why it is very difficult to think your way out of a panic attack for instance.

Your body doesn't think you need to do much thinking when a bloody great wild animal is jumping out at you. You don't need to go through much logical analysis to know you need to run as fast as you can?

So you only need a simple conscious thought when you feel like this. Accept this is nothing more that harmless sensations; both the feelings and thoughts are just part of the illusion. No matter how dark. You can control the level of thinking by just accepting this. Just accept the illusion and don't dwell on it.

Take the pressure off, take the foot of the pedal and then act on the next positive thought. Don't try too hard, just allow the penny to drop and keep practicing. Distract yourself if need be; don't take all this too seriously. Smile and know what it is, nothing serious, just moving up and down the lines of arousal and across the emotional system.

Do not try and spend ages thinking yourself out of sadness, dwelling on why you feel like this, analysing that harmless sensation in your tummy. Just accept the sensation as nothing important, acknowledge the unhelpful thoughts and then let them go, like a train passing through a train station. We all have this at different levels at different times in our lives; we just don't know how to talk about it. The funny thing is Leon, we are all worrying and trying to fix something, when in reality it just needs understanding. Not analysing.

We all need to take a breath and put the sword down. The more we take the pressure off, the more our mind clears. It then has the room to produce happier thoughts from our innate gifts of love and inner wisdom, from our higher levels of consciousness. We don't need to try and force this. We just need to get out of our own way and it happens automatically, as if by magic. Just practice Leon, don't test, just practice, before you know it you will end up on the fun side of the island nearly all the time.

Now lesson over, put your feet up and rest, I'll put on some fresh coffee and we can talk about this riddle of yours." The violinist smiled in a lovely caring way.

I did exactly as I was told. I sat down and put my feet up and waited for my coffee. I decided for the first time in forty years that there was somebody who may understand me.

I had heard this saying of losing the fear of fear many times in my therapy sessions, but I had never really understood it. Now I somehow felt different. Somehow, the violinist had given me the confidence to panic as much as I wanted to without worrying and then magically it all went away. Maybe this is what the magician was calling a paradox.

"So what did this Magician say to you Leon?" the violinist asked whilst serving coffee and oat biscuits.

I told the whole story to the violinist starting from the moment I first met the magician in the Old Goblin's Tavern going to the moment I left the boat. He listened with great interest, topping up our coffees and smiling every time he heard me mention Osclouro's fear trap.

When I finished, I was full of questions. I felt that the violinist had the answers. My first question referred to the playing card and riddle?

"Leon, the sacred deck carries many hidden secrets. There is a widely held misconception that the sacred deck is for gipsy fortune telling or something evil. In fact it carries more secrets of how the universe works and what we are doing here than any other manuscript in any of our worlds. Your Magician friend is a very clever man. He knows the meaning of the cards and the amazing learning they bring.

Everybody can sing if they find their song. The magician is referring to something buried in every human being, every animal, in fact every living thing. If you strip everything back, take away all the nonsense that life has thrown at us, all the things that we perceive to be important that are really nonsense, and come back to the pure and beautiful reason why we are living here today, then you will find your innate purpose in life. For you Leon, this is when you stop worrying about insignificant pressures and stop listening to anybody else. If you forget the made up expectations that are placed on you by society, family and so called people of authority and listen to the part of you that holds carefully your positive and loving purpose for being here. If you just stop thinking for a moment and trust your own intuition when it's staring you in the face.

Your innate purpose is always positive and always filled with happiness! Any dark thoughts that enter your head are just meaningless tests. These tests are there to help you. To test you until you find your song. And once you see it, nobody can knock you of your track. And fear and anxiety, well they become an old acquaintance from the past, totally undermined. Leon, Fear is replaced with love and happiness, starting with loving yourself." The violinist was still singing some of the words and making silly faces, but the message was clear.

I felt a warm feeling in my stomach, butterflies, but not the awful panicky butterflies that caused me so much distress. These were different they were lighter and felt more like excitement.

"Those feelings in your stomach are the same feelings of fear Leon. All that is happening is you are now thinking and feeling differently. That feeling is caused by adrenaline and energy moving around your body; it is nothing to be afraid of it's something to embrace. What you are feeling now is exactly the same sensation. The only difference is you are now receiving it with love and curiously rather than fear and despair." The violinist picked up the violin and started to play a familiar tune.

"Leon, it is you and only you that matters. If you are happy, then the people around are happy. If you love yourself then you will project that on everybody around you. What's important is you and your innate purpose in life. You make the choices, there is no external force or external illnesses, nothing horrible out there, no panic disorder and depressions that are hereditary or are bestowed upon us. We learn to take a particular path and sometimes we just need to slightly change direction. Anybody can do this, in any situation, at any age, with any history. We have the choice Leon. You have that choice. Everybody can sing if they find their song. Your song is your innate purpose" The violinist played a short magical tune on the violin so beautiful that it gave Leon goose pimples.

"Wow" said Ruby. "What an amazing way to look at life."

"Yes Ruby, sort of puts everything into perspective doesn't it?" Leon replied.

"Well yes, I guess it does, but it's totally unrealistic in my world" Ruby said.

"In what way Ruby?" Leon raised his head and looked into Ruby's eyes.

"Well, I don't live in this magical world of yours. I have to get up and go to work every day. My bills are piling up. I have pressure when meeting people. I cannot do anything or go anywhere without feeling panicky. Some mornings I wake up depressed without even knowing why? My mother and father don't understand me. I cannot be in an intimate relationship with anybody so I cannot even start to find love. I feel totally alone and totally misunderstood. I hate myself, I hate the way I look and I hate my life. I lost my childhood to worry; I lost my teenage years to depression and I'm now in my early forties, with no husband, no children and I'm angry. Angry this happened to me and continues to happen to me. Why didn't it happen to anybody else! I'm tired Leon. My purpose is now just survival and finding a little bit of enjoyment in the things that don't cause me fear or depression. This is now me. I feel protected and just want to be left alone. That's my choice."

"Yes Ruby you're right. It is your choice. Let me ask you something. Are you not just a little bit curious why all this may be happening to you?" Leon asked.

"Yes. Why me?" Ruby replied shedding a tear.

"Ruby, because you are destined for great things. You are ready to move up the levels of consciousness. All that you just said is just your current thoughts. They are just thoughts; that are travelling through your current belief filters. These thoughts then translate into what you say and the way you are choosing to live your life. Ruby, these thoughts are not real. When did thoughts ever reflect reality?"

"I don't understand?" Ruby said through her tears.

"I take my friend to watch a football game. I support the red team. I have supported them all my life. My friend supports the blue team. He follows them everywhere home and away. The blue team wins easily. They were brilliant. The red team were trash and didn't seem to try. My friend would be over the moon he would create the feelings of happiness. He would say it was a fantastic game and fantastic day. I however would say it was a terrible game, my team did not show up and the day was ruined"

"I don't understand your point. I hate football," Ruby replied a little annoyed.

"Well was it a good game or not Ruby?" Leon asked picking up the light off the edge of the bar.

"Well it depends on who you supported I guess" Ruby shrugged.

"What is the reality Ruby?"

Ruby looked confused.

"There is no reality Ruby, just our thoughts and beliefs creating the picture of reality that we experience. I watched the game through my thoughts and beliefs and my friend watched it though his thoughts and beliefs and we came up with a different outcome of emotions to the same event. At some stage in my past I decided to support the red team. I could change this at any time and it wouldn't make the slightest bit of difference to anybody else. It is not that important. I could also support the red team, and still enjoy every bit of the game without letting emotions get the most of me if I just shifted my thoughts and beliefs."

"But everything that has happened to me is true Leon. It is my reality" Ruby said.

"It was your reality Ruby, I'm not saying it wasn't, but it is only your reality. It isn't anybody else's, so does it really matter now? The past has gone, and it is now just sitting in the past of your unconscious mind in line with your thoughts and beliefs at that time. Just like the football game sitting in the past of my friend's unconscious mind in a different way to it sitting in the past of my unconscious mind. There is no reality, just the reality we create at the time. My friend will hold happy memories of the day and I if I choose to I will hold sad memories of the day. It will then sit in our past just like that, unless we revisit our memories and change our beliefs"

"I don't have any happy memories Leon?" Ruby said with tears streaming down her face.

Leon leant over and placed the light in Ruby's left hand and held her right hand.

"Well maybe now is a good time to start creating some Ruby" Leon smiled and nodded towards a wooden plaque propped up between the whisky bottles on the rear shelf of the bar.

Ruby raised her head and through the tears read the words,

You can create more in a day being yourself than one hundred years of being somebody else. Ancient Eth proverb

"Ruby the past is the past. Why let your view of the past affect now. For what purpose? For whose benefit? You can stop struggling now. Your fighting days are over. Put your sword down Ruby and just start being yourself; being anything else is a strain." Leon passed Ruby a tissue.

"Everything you've experienced so far has happened for a reason. You have a wonderful innate purpose Ruby. It's nobody else's purpose it's your purpose and it will bring peace and happiness" Leon squeezed Ruby's hand in a kind supportive way.

Ruby felt her shoulders drop as some of the heavy burden of life seemed to lift from her tired shoulders. OK how do I find the real me?

6 THE SCULPTURE

"So your song is your innate purpose Leon. Now you understand the riddle, all you need to do is find your path," the violinist relaxed into his seat and placed the playing card on the table.

"Where would I find it?" I asked.

The violinist chuckled and pointed at his heart "right here."

"There is not much left there" I sighed.

"Which is why you need to continue your quest Leon," the violinist leaned forward and for the first time looked serious. "You need to find Osclouro's fear trap."

The magician had already explained the paradox of Osclouro's fear trap, letting the sensations of fear in and also waving them goodbye, a combination that could not be processed by the conscious mind, so how would this help me find my innate purpose?

"Osclouro the Thirtieth is an amazing wizard who lives hundreds of miles from here in a castle on the outer rim of Mount Orr. He or she carries the eternal wisdom, which is passed down from generation to generation. Osclouro's fear trap merges the secret message of the sacred deck with the natural elements of the universe. It carries the simple guide to replace fear with love and brings balance and empowerment to everybody who seeks it" the violinist continued to play beautiful music.

"Where can I find it Fergus?" I asked.

The violinist nodded at the playing card faced down on the table and then drifted away back towards his tent pirouetting with his violin.

I looked down at the playing card. Don't tell me the Musician card had some other message in it that would tell me where I need to go next. I had stared at that card for hours on the boat and could find nothing. It was only the violinist who could make any sense of it and he had already told me what it means.

I turned over the card and nearly fell off my seat. I was no longer looking at the musician card I was staring at a man and women hold holding hands. I was the looking at the lover's card.

"Get ready Leon. I need to show you something" the violinist came out of his tent wearing a safari jacket and was busily packing his bag with provisions.

"Where are we going," I asked.

"To show you the fear trap," the violinist said nonchalantly

"What to the mountain to see the wizard?" I was shocked by the suggestion.

"No Leon, no need for that. You will be done by supper" the violinist responded whilst pulling his packed bag over his shoulder "Let's go."

I quickly grabbed some water and spare clothes and followed the violinist into the woods. Our trusty violin followed behind silently.

The violinist knew every bit of the woods; he waved at every animal and nodded at every plant as we walked by. He stopped every now and then to show me something of interest. He loved the woods and everything thing that was in it. It was lovely to see.

We had been walking for around an hour before the violinist stopped and put in his bag down on the path. He pulled out some fruit and shared it with me.

"We need to head off the path, in this direction," the violinist pointed diagonally ahead between the trees.

We set off into the wood mud squelching under our feet. The air was fresh and smelt of pine leaves. The odd sound of deer darting away in the distance and birds flying out of the trees overhead was all that could be heard. The violinist was quiet and absolutely focused on the task in hand. I liked this side of Fergus.

After several hours the violinist eventually spoke. "Not long now Leon." We made our way down a gradual bank towards a small clearing in the trees. When we reached the centre of the clearing we put down our bags and sat down to rest for few moments.

We sat in silence, regaining our breath. The violinist seemed to be meditating, the violin sat silently by Fergus's side. I didn't want to disturb his concentration so just sat quietly looking into the trees ahead. The violinist broke the silence with a quiet whisper.

"Five minutes in that direction Leon you will find a small opening to a cave. In the cave you will see a small stream running through it. Follow that stream to reach an underground rock pool lit up by its natural plantation. To the right of the pool there will be a passageway leading to an underground tomb, the tomb of Osclouro the First. Within the tomb Leon you will find a sculpture carved into the rock face. Find the round spot of light on the ground and sit down and face the sculpture. When you are complete come back and meet me here. I will wait for you." The violinist lay back and closed his eyes.

I thought for a few seconds and then opened my mouth to ask my first question. I hesitated. The violinist was already starting to drift off to sleep making snoring noises. It was no good asking him anything he had been clear. It's up to me now.

I collected a few things from my bag, a bottle of water, torch, and waterproof jacket and then made my way into the woods once again. As I left the clearing Fergus uttered something in his sleep. "Remember Leon, stop thinking."

I looked at my watch and then checked every thirty seconds as I steadily walked forward ensuring I held my line. In no time at all I was staring at a small cave carved out of a rock face smothered by bushes and branches.

I turned on the torch and made my way to the opening of the cave. I was nervous, sweating and shaking, but not panicking. Since the episode back at the tent that morning my sensations of fear had not been strong enough to create a full-blown panic attack. I was very uncomfortable, but felt in control. "Here goes," I whispered.

The cave was lighter than I expected, there was natural light coming in from cracks in the walls. The first part of the cave was airy with the roof of the cave extending to at least five metres high. A stream ran through a tunnel at the far end. I followed the stream and walked steadily down a gradual slope.

It only took me a minute or two to reach the underground rock pool, which as the violinist had said, was lit up naturally. I looked to the right of the pool and saw the passageway. It was darker in the passageway my torch became my main source of light.
Amazingly I was more curious than nervous. I had nearly reached the tomb, which would hopefully unlock Osclouro's message.

I noticed light at the end of the passageway, the butterflies in my stomach returned and I started to breathe more quickly. These are only sensations, just accept them for what they are I thought. Use them as excitement and embrace them. I carried on forward towards the light. There were eight large steps leading down into the tomb. I started to walk down the steps, eight, seven, six, going deeper into the cave. The sensations of fear stayed with me, but they somehow felt different. Fear became excitement; my light-headed feeling became dreamy. Five, four deeper still. With every step I seemed to become even more relaxed. It was a strange feeling but also a wonderful feeling. The pins and needles in my arms felt more tingly and shiny rather than distressing and restricting. Three, two deeper still, I felt like my body had floated away just leaving my soul to drift down the final steps, my vision was blurred, I couldn't feel my legs. I was relaxed and sleepy as I went deeper, one and then zero. I was in the tomb of Osclouro the First.

The tomb was large and square shaped. The walls and ceiling were smooth, the floor was carefully ridged to provide grip under foot. Shining natural light from holes in the walls lit the tomb up in bright colours of green and blue. A large stone coffin was positioned to one side with an engraving of the words *Osclouro the first, thank you for sharing with us this special stage in your magnificent journey.*

On the far wall, was the sculpture engraved from floor to ceiling into the rock, incredibly clear and painted in beautiful colours. I stared at it for a moment and felt an immediate sense of relaxation and contentment. A shining light from a hole in the ceiling shone down to make a circle in the centre of the floor, just like the violinist had said.

I positioned my jacket on the floor and took a drink of water. I turned off my torch and sat down to face the sculpture. The adrenaline that had flowed through my body causing me so much discomfort in the past was flowing through my body with the same intensity, but with a totally different feel. I felt incredible. I couldn't explain why the same symptoms were now making me feel totally different and really didn't care. I just enjoyed the feeling.

The sculpture was just magnificent. It started with a large circle in the centre. The circle was split into four segments with a heart shape in the middle. Within in each segment there was a picture followed by a word engraved in the ancient language of Eth.

Below the picture were two figures one male and one female. The male figure was giving a set of golden keys to the female figure. The female figure was looking upwards towards a beautiful image of a god like figure above the circle with welcoming arms extending outwards.

There was a stream of light coming through a small hole at the back of the tomb shining over the figure, which was covered in beautiful golden colours. I could not make out whether it was male or female, but it looked truly beautiful and contented. He or She was giving a loving smile to the female. "An angel from the heavens," I whispered.

I brought my attention back to the circle and to the picture in the first segment. It was a violin and wand resting on top of a planet. A simple picture stained in a brown and green colour. The Ancient Eth word underneath translated into ground.

In the segment to the right the colours were totally different. A beautiful mix of blue, green and pink. Three wavy lines in dark blue were carved into the rock with the word peace engraved.

The third segment in the bottom left; carried a picture of a monk and the numerals one and two with an infinity sign floating above. The word energy was carved into the rock.

In the final segment there was a knight riding on a dragon breathing fire with the word power alongside.

Around the heart, smaller letters spelt out the words "Accept, acknowledge, breathe and let it go."

On the outside of the circle was a swirling set of rings with an arrow pointing upwards. Within the swirling rings I could make out images of faces smiling and also images of faces with devil like features.

There were no more words and no more pictures. This was Osclouro's fear trap, now to piece together what it meant. How will it repair my life and how it will lead me to my innate purpose?

I sat and stared at the sculpture for some time. It was as if it was talking to me, trying to help me unlock its secret message. I started in the left hand segment. OK a violin and a wand on top of a planet with the word ground carved into the rock. Maybe this refers to the magician and violinist that I had spent the last few days with. Fergus has already helped me dissolve a severe panic attack and led me to this wonderful place, but what did the planet represent and how did the world ground fit in?

The second segment containing the word peace seemed simpler. The three purple lines surely represented water and the colours of greens and pinks were relaxing. This was surely a message around calmness. The irony of this was that I was scared stiff of water, I thought.

The third segment was a complete mystery, with the Monk, the two and one numerals and the infinity sign. The word energy must have some link to these images.

The final segment again seemed simple, a fire breathing dragon with the word power. This must be something to do with finding the strength and power to overcome things.

My focus then moved to the heart shape in the centre of the circle. The shape was filled with glass and was dark inside. The words were carved in silver in the rock in the wall "
"Accept, acknowledge, breathe and let it go."

This must refer to symptoms or sensations of fear, just like the Magician had said. Accept that the symptoms you feel during fear are just sensations. Let it go must mean relax and let things happen? Does that sound right? Why would this be in a heart shape? I assume the heart refers to love. A thought then popped into my head from my unconscious mind. "When you stop fearing and start loving the world, your world will stop fearing and start loving you." The words that accompanied the letter I received three days ago. Is this connected in some way?

I took a sip of water and shifted my focus to the male and female images. The male image was passing golden keys to the female image, which was looking up to the angel in the sky. They appeared to some way be connecting to each other. Male connecting to female and female connecting to the angel. The angel was beautifully carved, showing the features of a happy and contented face. Something was telling me that this had something to do with different bodies or minds of a person being balanced and connected in some way. In a spiritual way maybe? The swirling circles moving upwards with smiling faces maybe represented happiness and progression. That would make sense, but what about the devil faces. Overall I was confused. How could I work all this out, just sitting here staring at this collage of images.

I felt myself getting frustrated. Why can't someone just bloody tell me what this is all about? Trying to guess what the Magician and Violinist were actually saying was like playing charades with my mad auntie Janet at Christmas.

"Remember Leon, stop thinking" that was the violinist's parting words. He was telling me to stop thinking logically. OK I will just sit here and meditate on the image I guess. I stared at the image and tried to turn off my mind talk. The light shining onto the image from the hole in the back of the cave was now moving down towards the top of the circle as the sun was beginning to drop.

All of a sudden, I felt very sleepy, not an uncomfortable tired feeling, but a very relaxed sleepy feeling. What is happening to me? I have hardly got the energy to lift my arms and take a drink I thought. The room became darker, apart from the light shining onto the image, which was now travelling down towards the centre of the circle.

I could hear the sound of my breathing. My eyelids became very heavy. The muscles around my eyes and my face became very relaxed as I slowly sank into my cushioned jacket on the floor.

I felt more and more dreamy, all the muscles in my body began to relax. My eyelids began to close. I sank deeper and deeper into my jacket. What a wonderful feeling, I was falling into a dream. As my eyelids were just about to shut completely, the light flashed directly onto the heart shape in the centre of the circle, and lit up the sculpture in a beautiful display of light.

The heart shape was now displaying a mirror reflection of me. Three rays of light were connecting my mirror image to the two figures below and the angel figure above. The rings around the circle seem to be making a swirling movement and the images and words in the four segments of the sculpture were even more clear and pronounced.

It was beautiful.

The Fear Trap

"Wow. Were you not scared at all?" asked Ruby.

"No. It is really hard to explain Ruby, but after forty years of anxiety and depression and I had never felt anything like this before. It was pure relaxation, curiosity without fear, an emptiness without negative thoughts" Leon replied as if he was associating back into the moment.

"What happened next Leon, did you get the answer to the fear trap?" Ruby continued.

"Well yes and no I guess" Leon replied.

Ruby looked perplexed.

Leon continued, "I got the answer at the logical level. It actually came to me in a matter of seconds, I have no idea where from."

"Wow. Would you share it with me?" Ruby asked.

"I will share it with you Ruby if you promise just one thing" Leon looked serious.

Ruby nodded.

"Please promise me Ruby that you will follow your own meaning and your own journey. You will stop trying to force your solution based on what you currently believe or may have read or been told and will start accepting the sensations and thoughts in a positive way by choosing your own path."

"Why is that important to you Leon?' Ruby asked.

"You will stand on my shoulders and transform the world" Leon smiled.

Ruby felt warm inside. "Leon, you said you only got the answer at the logical level, but the magician said to you that change happens at the unconscious level?"

"That is correct Ruby, if you believe in the unconscious mind. Do you?" Leon replied.

"I don't know" Ruby answered as she sipped her drink.

"Well which one of your minds decided to bring that cup to your mouth to take a drink?"

"I consciously decided to do that, my mouth was dry," Ruby replied.

"Great, that makes perfect sense, but were you also consciously moving every muscle in your arm to take the cup and move it towards your mouth? This movement is already programmed into your mind and body. You did it without thinking. Just like when you drive a car or walk down the road. If you tried to instruct every movement in your body through conscious thinking, then you would have to instruct every single one of your hundreds of muscles just to move one arm or leg. This would prove impossible so something takes over." Leon paused for a moment and then continued.

"The automatic sensations of panic and fear are held at a deeper level, so it makes sense to overcome them at a deeper level. When you are highly sensitised your unconscious mind can become trigger-happy and release energy to prepare your body for danger. These sensations are harmless but also very distressing when they are out of context. Conscious logical thinking is also very difficult when ninety percent of your body is consumed dealing with a panic attack or bout of depression."

"So how do you also train your deeper mind then?" Ruby asked.

"This is where Osclouro's fear trap comes into play Ruby. It shows the way to overcome anxiety and move forward to a purposeful happy life. However, as I was to learn, to embrace the learnings and empower yourself at all levels you go on your own journey of discovery." Leon replied.

"I want to go on my journey. I'm sick of my condition. Leon can you please show me?" Ruby asked desperately.

"Yes I will show you Ruby. From now on as I tell my story, stop thinking. Certainly don't bother thinking you have some condition. Does it really help if you think that? Remember Ruby, thoughts are just thoughts. You cannot stop them from popping into your head, but you can choose which ones to act upon. Acknowledge them and then let them float away. Only act on the ones that come from the higher level of consciousness thinking. It soon becomes the new habit. You only need a few practices to program the new path in the body and mind.

If you feel fearful, panicky, stressed or upset then use your ten percent that you have left to repeat the words in the centre of the sculpture. Accept, acknowledge, breathe and let it go, or better still create your own mantra. Ask yourself for the mantra that works for you, it will be sitting there in your higher levels of consciousness, in your innate wisdom waiting for you to access it.

Put no pressure on feeling better. It doesn't matter if you feel better or not, just repeat the words and carry on listening to me. Is that OK Ruby," Leon asked.

"I'm in!" Ruby smiled. It was the first time she had found some hope in many years. The pressure of dealing with her terrifying issues seemed to be dissolving for the time being.

"Great, and remember to go on your own journey," Leon reminded Ruby. "Now where was I?"

"Osclouro's Fear Trap, the sculpture," reminded Ruby.

"Yes that's right the sculpture"

"I was in a relaxing daze, staring at the sculpture and the whole message came to me like an ultra-fast computer download. The message was to completely change my life and show me my innate personal wisdom and happiness. As it will for everybody who embraces it and everybody who follows the rest of my story, including you Ruby."

7 LEGEND OF OSCLOURO

A thousand years ago, a young king ruled the land of Eth. It was a difficult time. Seasons of bad weather had destroyed the harvest and food was scarce. There were many poor people in the kingdom and everybody was living in fear.

The king was upset and worried about his people. His attempts to turn around the situation had failed and all he could see was a bleak future for his kingdom.

The king's brother was angry. He had the responsibility for collecting taxes and was not prepared to accept the decline in funds. He became more and more angry with the people in the kingdom for their lack of success and decided to take charge of the situation.

He ordered the king's army to threaten the people if taxes were not paid in full and on time, striking fear across the kingdom. As the kingdom continued to struggle the army administered many terrifying tortures to force the people into action.

The young king was not aware of his brother's actions, but over time became suspicious of his brother's methods. He was worried about his brother's health and state of mind. He seemed to be deteriorating each day.

One day the king ventured out of the palace in disguise and into a local village. He could feel the emotions and stress flowing through his people as he walked through the streets. He then witnessed a young farmer being tortured by an army major. The king was shocked and saddened by what he had witnessed.

The king was upset that he had allowed this to happen to his people and immediately confronted his brother. His brother was angry and hateful. He called the king a coward and threatened to overthrow the kingdom. They fought with each other over the coming weeks, until the king could no longer allow the situation to continue. They were both angry, driven to hate and fearful of losing their power and status.

The king recalled the army from the villages of the kingdom and told them to hand in their weapons until he and his brother had resolved their dispute. The health of his brother worsened as the anger and hate set in.

Several months passed and the kingdom continued to suffer. Food was scarcer than it had been and the people were tired and weak. The torture had finished, but the energy had been sucked out of the people. Moreover, they were fearful that the darker days of torture would return.

On one very dark morning a gypsy entered the kingdom and insisted on speaking to the king. After much persuading the king agreed to see the traveller and listened to his story with great curiosity.

The Gypsy told the story of an incredible wizard called Osclouro who lived in the outer rim of Mount Orr. This wizard produced success and happiness for anybody who believed in him.

The king was intrigued by the gypsy and his story and invited the wizard to the kingdom to try and help him. The wizard agreed to meet the king and listened carefully to the story of the demise of his kingdom.

He then asked the king for a private area within the kingdom and instructed that he must not be disturbed for a period of fourteen days. The king agreed.

The wizard gathered the most fearful, depressed and who most people thought were the weakest people in the kingdom to the palace and spent fourteen days training them in the ancient secrets of his magical world. Nobody was allowed to make contact with the wizard or his new apprentices during this time.

On the morning of the fifteenth day he then sent the apprentices back into the kingdom, to work and teach alongside the people in the towns and villages.

The apprentices had gone through a massive transformation. They were no longer fearful, no longer panicking and no longer depressed.

They were determined and motivated. They spread hope and happiness across the kingdom by delivering a feeling of beautiful magic everywhere they ventured.

Each day the apprentices worked together with the people to replant the crops with richer soils, fish in busier waters and work together to rebuild the kingdom. Within no time the kingdom and people became happy and rich once again.

Over time the brother released his anger and became a compassionate member of the kingdom leadership. He rebuilt his loving relationship with the king and resumed his duties.

The king often asked the wizard what had happened during those fourteen days, to which the wizard would always just reply "we broke the fear-trap." The wizard worked in partnership with the king in the palace for many more happy years.

Legend has it that on the wizard's hundredth birthday he announced to the king in a private meeting that he was going to pass over to the other side and would disappear for a few days in preparation. He then asked the king to prepare a funeral with his close friends in a small cave in a wood a thousand miles away. The king and a small convoy of the wizard's friends and family including his beautiful wife Lola and son Osclouro the second journeyed to the cave to celebrate the wizard's life.

It was said the wizard had already made his own tomb and left a beautiful sculpture on the cave wall. The king engraved the words *Osclouro the first, thank you for sharing with us this special stage of your magnificent journey* in memory of his best friend.

"This was the sculpture I was staring at Ruby," Leon said "Lit up in beautiful light. This is what it said to me."

The violin and the wand on the planet with the word ground referred to being grounded. To learn at a conscious level that fear and depression create sensations in your body and mind that are just sensations, there is no need to fear or get upset by them. They are just a sign to say you are now ready to move up the levels of consciousness. The violin and the wand were pointing to the violinist and magician who are the current holders of the wisdom to learn the basic skills to dissolve anxiety, depression and fear.

The three purple lines in the second segment do indeed represent water. By using the peaceful sounds, the floating movement and calming freshness it is possible to find the peace in life that accompanies losing the fear of anxiety through being grounded. The beautiful colours of pink and green are the relaxing colours of the rainbow. When you have peace you also have the ability to love everything and anybody around you.

The third segment carrying the image of the monk, the one and two numbers and the infinity sign referred to the importance of breathing and creation of energy. The number one refers to the length of your inward breath and two to the outward breath. Once in, twice out. The infinity sign says energy is infinite; you can create as much as you want. The monk would be the holder of the wisdom to create fulfilment through positive energy.

The Knight and the fire-breathing dragon with the word power teach the art of building your own strength and power in your physical body. Turning adrenaline, which once caused discomfort, to adrenaline that builds strength and ambition. This will dissolve your fear and anxiety for good. The knight on the dragon is in control of the power and holds the key to connecting your mind and body to keep you strong. It also brings together the ambition of the modern world with higher level of consciousness thinking. They are not in conflict. You can be happy and with very few possessions and also happy with lots of possessions. You do not need to feel guilty chasing the treats of the modern world.

"The wizard left his final message to teach people how to dissolve fear," Ruby said.

"That's right Ruby simple, grounding through knowledge, peace through relaxing mediation, energy through breath and fire power" Leon replied.

"Ground, water, breath and fire power" Ruby whispered.

Leon smiled, "or translated into your world Ruby"

"Earth, water, air, fire," Ruby and Leon whispered together.

"So, the four elements hold the key to the solution?" Ruby suggested.

"Yes Ruby, carefully positioned in a circle. You see to follow the journey to dissolve anxiety it is no good having a one to ten step process because as you approach the end your fear will play tricks on you and will convince you that you have failed. The four segments are a continuous process. No pressure, no judgements and no measures. Just a calm and enjoyable lifestyle to build your knowledge, relaxation, energy and strength."

"I feel better just knowing that, but how do I know that I am making progress. That I'm getting better? That I will not fall back into a terrible place." Ruby asked.

"Good point. I thought the same Ruby. Think about it Ruby. There is no terrible place. There just is. The more our thinking describes the duality of a condition and a solution, the more it puts pressure on and the more we get caught in the fear trap, with all its measures and judgements. It is an illusion. An illusion based on the thoughts we choose to act on. Just be you and take all of you on the journey to the higher levels of consciousness. The answer is hidden in the swirling circles cloaked around the segments," Leon continued.

"The swirling circles represent your path and it's always fine, no matter what is happening. There are happy faces and devil faces;

these represent the good times and bad times, the happy times and the distressing times. There are no judgements or measures around either of these. Both are good when it comes to moving forward. Both give positive learning."

"I don't understand. How can acute anxiety be a good thing? It sends you backwards not forwards?" Ruby said confused.

"This is the whole misconception of your world Ruby. Failure is treated in a way that suggests a backward movement. It is wrong. All learning is good it defines you. It allows you to develop. It helps you unveil the amazing you that is always there. Loving, compassionate and wise with innate wellbeing. When you suffer from panic or anxiety write down everything. How you feel, how you think and later follow up with recording a positive learning to lift another veil," Leon said.

"How can I get a positive learning out of such a terrible thing?" Ruby asked.

"It becomes easy with practice Ruby, believe me. Once you start to think in this way. The fear trap becomes obvious and your misery and anxiety starts to dissolve as you take your positive learning and continue to pure happiness."

"Are you sure you have this right Leon?" Ruby asked suspiciously.

"Yes Ruby one hundred percent sure. I am also one hundred percent sure you will not believe it. When you are suffering your fear plays tricks on you. It is part of your thinking habit. Your habit will tell you that you are going backwards. I am not forcing you to believe that you are only really one thought away from the happy and relaxed you. Your setbacks are not really setbacks; they are just more positive learning. You only need to practice once and suddenly feel a slight change to your old habit and everything then changes for ever. It only takes more practice, not testing, just practice and the new learning and thinking becomes the new habit." Leon moved the light closer to Ruby.

"OK Pretty inspiring" said Ruby.

"Yes, but you are still missing something Ruby?"

"Yes Leon. What I have is worse than that. It cannot be solved through something as simple as some clever sayings. You don't fully understand" Ruby said.

Leon chuckled and held Ruby's right hand tightly.

"Ruby. I know this is what you are thinking. Do you really think after forty years of suffering I sat in front of a sculpture and was convinced myself? Remember a paradox cannot be processed by the conscious mind."

Leon smiled and gave Ruby a friendly wink.

"Ruby you are not alone anymore. You were never alone. We are partners on a journey of discovery. No pressure, no measures and no expectation. Put the sword down Ruby and It will just come from within you."

"What is this journey Leon?" Ruby asked, starting to feel a bit better.

"The journey to happiness, the journey to the higher levels of consciousness. It doesn't need to be a struggle to find it because it is always there. We just need to unveil it," Come along Ruby, it will be fun.

"So, was this your innate purpose Leon?" Ruby asked.

"Well part of it Ruby. The full picture was still not clear so I studied the remainder of the sculpture."

I looked at the centre of the sculpture at my face reflecting back in a heart shaped mirror. This was simply suggesting I love myself. Not partially, but truly loving of myself. Turning all my issues, failings, and disappointments into a loving positive journey. Taking a new perspective. To stop beating myself up for not meeting expectations imposed on me by society, family, friends, partners and also more importantly by myself. Love myself as a human being and be proud of my journey so far.

The rays of light shining from my image to the male figure, female figure and angel in the sky was connecting the conscious being, the deeper being and the spiritual being.

The male figure represents our conscious being where we logically think and communicate. The conscious being is handing the golden keys to the female being who represents the deeper being or deeper mind. This is where we hold our values and beliefs about ourselves. The female figure is then looking towards the angel in the sky who represents our spiritual being.

Our conscious mind communicates with our deeper mind and our deeper mind connects to our spiritual mind. So when everybody keeps saying stop thinking they mean turn off the logical mind. Your deeper mind communicates with your spiritual mind when you are meditating.

The male is handing the female the golden keys, so the conscious mind is handing loving instructions to the deeper mind. The golden keys are also being received by the deeper mind to unlock the messages from your spiritual mind.

"And Ruby it is your spiritual mind which carries your innate purpose. The angel is smiling because your innate purpose is always beautiful and positive. This is the true you. It is always there."

"This is a lot to take on" Ruby was desperately trying to keep up.

"I'm sorry Ruby. Forgive me for talking too much. Choose to ignore or reframe the bits that are just too much at this stage."

Ruby somehow felt more at peace and thought that she could at least start to pass on positive messages through her thinking mind if nothing else. That makes perfect sense. Also stop creating all this expectation and pressure. I'm sick of doing that she thought.

Leon observed Ruby and smiled.

"Did you manage to find the rest of your innate purpose Leon?" Ruby asked.

"I knew I had to experience my own journey. I also knew that it was already there inside, it was only I that could get in my own way me, I just needed to lift the covers and I was looking forward to it," Leon replied.

"And your innate purpose?" Ruby asked again.

"All I thought at that stage was how long I'd been meditating in this beautiful cave and would my friend Fergus still be waiting for me outside?" Leon then continued to tell Ruby how he had made his way back out of the tomb and out of the cave into the fresh air outside.

It was dusk. The five-minute walk seemed to take longer on the way back. I seemed to be walking taller and with more purpose, but definitely slower. As I approached the clearing I was filled with a warm feeling of joy, as I saw Fergus proudly sitting on a tree stump playing a beautiful tune on his violin.

"Hello Fergus"

"Did you find the answer to the fear trap Leon?" Fergus asked.

"I think so" I replied "thank you for bringing me here."

"Don't mention it. Now it's time to say goodbye my friend. Your boat is only a ten minute walk in that direction. My dogs very kindly brought your bags from the tent and have dropped them into your boat. You may have to wipe off the slobber, but apart from that you are good to go. If you set sail tonight you can be in Anatonia in the morning."

"Anatonia? No please I don't want to go anywhere else. I'm happy to spend some more time here and then make my way home to enjoy my life with my new learnings?" I said desperately.

"As much as I love your company Leon, your adventure is still in its infancy. It is now time to embrace the true magic of Osclouro" Fergus smiled.

"How do I do that?" I replied

"You experience and live it. You integrate the magic of Osclouro into your life. You keep a smile on your face and allow the happiness to exist. And more important than ever you embrace the setbacks" Fergus pointed intently.

"I'm not sure Fergus. This all seems easy for you. You spend your days without a care in the world. You are naturally jolly and relaxed. Always happy! Your life is not filled with fear, anger, guilt or sadness. I however still have a long way to go to make up for all the years I have suffered in fear. Back at home I have debts to pay, a difficult accounting job that I'm forced to do at home. I fear the outside world and have nobody who seems to understand or care about me."

The violinist laid down his violin on the ground in silence and for the first time walked away disconnected from the instrument. He walked towards the edge of the clearing and slowly turned round to face me. He gently nodded and beckoned me with his finger.

I followed in silence.

We walked several minutes back towards the direction of the cave, but instead of entering took a right turn towards some large rocks positioned in a circle. The violinist entered the circle and bowed his head as if to be paying his respects.

The area was peaceful. It was if nobody knew this part of the wood apart from Fergus. It seemed to be his special place.

I looked ahead and noticed two small rock shapes nestled into the ground. They were surrounded by beautiful flowers; pink roses, cream lilies and colourful heathers. The air was filled with sweetness. The gentle breeze mixed the scents into an aromatic calming atmosphere.

As we both got closer, I noticed that the two small rocks were carved into arched shapes and had neat writing carved into the rock. I knelt in front of the stones and began to read the words.

One had a name of Louisa and one had a name of Jacob both neatly carved. I looked closely at the words beneath – Louisa my never-ending love and best friend passed over aged thirty eight. Jacob. May peace and happiness stay with you my beautiful and wonderful son, passed over aged twelve. I will always love you both more than words will ever describe.

I was looking at two gravestones

As I looked at Fergus a huge amount of sadness suddenly consumed my body. He was kneeling at the gravestone with tears streaming down his face.

This was his family.

"You see Leon. We were the perfect family, full of love and fun. Louisa was my childhood sweetheart; we went through schooling and college together and were never apart. After we married we had a beautiful son. You should have seen him Leon. He was kind, happy and clever. He used to love playing tricks on Louisa and me. He was always up to some mischief, but we didn't mind because his heart was always in the right place. The three of us had an unbreakable bond; we truly loved each other."

Fergus was grimacing and shaking his head. He had placed himself right back into his memories.

"For several months Louisa had mentioned to me about having our chimney cleaned. I had it on my busy to-do-list, but somehow never got round to it. One night whilst I was out at my regular bridge evening I bumped into the chimney sweeper and arranged for him to come over and have a look the following day."

Fergus looked down and breathed in forcefully to build the strength for the next sentence.

"When I returned home that night, I could smell fumes from outside my door. I burst the front door open to find my house filled with thick black smoke. I pulled out Louisa and Jacob onto the street outside and tried everything to breathe life back into them, but it was no good, I was too late. I had lost them."

I stared at Fergus in shock, full of sorrow.

"You see Leon, the chimney that night had blocked the fumes from leaving the room and Louisa and Jacob had drifted off to sleep, cuddled up in each other's arms on the sofa. I was just too late. They were never to wake up from that sleep"

"Oh Fergus, I am so sorry."

Fergus continued….

"For several years I retreated from life. Drowned in guilt and hurt. I had no motivation to go on living. I hated everything and everybody. Most of all I hated myself. Day after day I just drifted through a dark and lonely life, recounting the events of that night. Trying to make sense of it. I was angry, hurt and filled with tremendous guilt. I kept saying to myself if only I had listened to Louisa earlier and cleared out that damn chimney, then Louisa and Jacob would still be here laughing, playing and sharing in the beautiful life we had."

"You could not have known Fergus, it is one of just one of those awful accidents," I said with sympathetic tears.

Fergus bowed his head, closed his eyes and then fought back his tears, he took a deep breath and then slowly raised his head and focused his attention on me.

"Then one day, a stranger knocked on my door and demanded that I let him in. I resisted but he was insistent. Eventually I gave in and he came into my home. The stranger turned out to be some sort of magician a very odd fellow who was determined to help me.

I had not been in close contact with anybody since Louisa and Jacob had passed away. The only people who were close to me were very uncomfortable in my company and had resigned to sending me the odd letter of sympathy or desperately trying to get me professional help. There were also some people who somehow felt sorry for me and blamed me at the same time. Louisa's mother would look at me with such sad eyes that it would amplify my guilt to a level that words just could not describe.

You see, there was nobody who could help me Leon, because I didn't want to be helped. I was afraid that if I released just one small piece of my sadness or guilt then I would be letting Louisa and Jacob down even more.

The magician had been looking for me for several months. He had heard my story from somebody anonymous in the higher council of doctors and magicians. He was different from anybody who has spoken to me before. He was sympathetic, but did not dwell on sympathy. He also listened. I mean really listened. He did not attempt to change my thoughts; he just listened and acknowledged them.

He continually asked whether he could stay for longer with me. I was reluctant but eventually gave in. The magician ended up staying with me for exactly fourteen days"

Just like Osclouro's apprentices I thought.

"During that time, we shared everything. Our emotions, thoughts, beliefs and values. I started to see the world and our existence in this particular world differently."

The magician taught me to find my innate purpose. I had to dig deep to find it and when I did everything seemed to change. The world through my eyes looked different. My world looked different. I could not change the past, but I could change the present and I was about to change the future for many people who were going through their own seemingly impossible journeys.

My innate purpose Leon was to help people. To help as many people as possible to live without fear, without guilt, without anger and without continuous sadness. He had chosen me because I had been to the depths of despair. I knew what it was like to go to places worse than anybody could ever imagine. Because of this I could help even more people by teaching and embracing the wisdom of Osclouro."

"How? How could you find the strength to do this, when you feel so responsible for ending the life of your loved ones?"

"Louisa and Jacob are still here in my heart, in my dreams and in my life. I now feel them pushing me along, supporting me, helping me. The love just gets stronger and the negative emotions now sit in a chapter in the past where they rightfully belong. I cannot help people and the planet, whilst I carried those destructive emotions."

He stood up and wiped away his tears.

"I learnt how to be brave, to only listen to people who generally wanted to help me with helping others. I stopped accepting the negative projections of others. Those people who would project their own anger, guilt and fear into my world. I stopped taking on all the issues and decided to help them too."

He looked directly into my eyes.

"I learnt to move forward no matter what. To not judge the world and everybody in it. I wiped away the negative emotion shackles and found the loving, compassionate person that was waiting patiently for me."

He walked over and stroked the two gravestones.

"Leon, I visit Louisa and Jacob every day here. That is my moment with my family. I sometimes choose to be sad and then when I leave this place I continue my journey in true happiness."

Fergus walked over and pointed at the playing card in my top pocket. He smiled kindly.

"You cannot help anybody or add anything to the evolvement of this chapter of your life, if you sit staring at yourself in self-pity and misery. None of us fully understand why things happen. Remember the swirling lines always moving forward no matter what? We will always be tested. It's the road we choose when the test happens that's important, so keep smiling young Leon."

"Do you think it's my innate purpose to help people, to teach them to rise above fear and be happy" I asked.

Fergus patted me on the shoulder and nodded. "Yes I do Leon." I felt myself wanting to embrace this great man. Fergus responded and we hugged.

"It was at this moment that something shifted in me Ruby" Leon said.

Ruby had also been crying as Leon was reciting the story about the violinist. Leon continued.

"A burst of energy, of love and healing that filled my body and poured out of my heart towards Fergus. Something bigger than life, higher than this world and I felt it Ruby, in every bone, every muscle, every molecule in my body to the last fibre. An infinite energy of love and healing that I had never felt before" Leon smiled.

How can something so beautiful be born from something so terrible Ruby thought. She then hesitated and whispered to herself lines from the poem "IF" by Rudyard Kipling.

"If you can meet with triumph and disaster and treat those two impostors just the same"

I think something is slowly starting to sink in Ruby thought.

Leon warmly observed Ruby as he took a sip of his drink, he continued.

We then made our way back to the clearing.

"Where is Anatonia?" I asked Fergus.

"One hundred miles upstream. If you set off tonight, you will be there by lunchtime" Fergus replied as he reached for his violin.

"Must I go? Is it that important?" I added

"Leon. It is your choice of course. I somehow feel that you will have fun there. Sometimes it's good to just do things for fun. You deserve it" Fergus replied.

The tunes on the violin had started. They were calm and relaxing.

"Will you come with me?" I asked hopefully as I pulled my bag over my shoulder.

"I would love to come Leon, but have promised to build new stables for the reverend next week and anyway who would look after the dogs whilst I was away. I have to plan my trips some time in advance. I'm in big demand in these woods you know" Fergus replied.

"Anyway. It will be better for you to go alone on this particular adventure. Anatonia is the land of dreams. Enjoy it my good friend."

"Will I see you again?"

"Only if you remember to bring your ticket," Fergus winked.

Fergus extended his hand "Leon, in the city of Eth, there is a street called Eth Street that sits at the highest point in the city, at the peak with views over the harbour. You will have to face something here. This will break the fear trap once and for all."

We shook hands. Leon pointed in the direction of the sailboat and then danced away into the trees with his trusty violin. "Remember if you haven't visited Eth Street you haven't lived. There is no need to be afraid."

Everything was silent and I was once again alone. I was going to miss my good friend.

8 LAND OF DREAMS

The sailboat was exactly how I had left it. As I approached the lights flicked on and the horn sounded. It seemed pleased to see me.

I was able to board the boat comfortably; my fear of the boat had disappeared. My fear of water was still there, so I avoided looking over the side and made my way to the cabin.

I felt the boat nudge away from the edge and the engine start to rumble. It was starting to get dark; I snuggled up into some blankets in the hammock. My mind was racing with the events of the day. I was now feeling excited. I could not remember when I had felt excitement without it being superseded by fear. Anatonia here I come I thought before I drifted off to sleep.

Ruby took a slow deep breath and looked down at her rucksack. It was still and calm.

"I feel very relaxed Leon. I do not understand it. Why can't I feel like this all the time?" Ruby said.

"You can Ruby. Your emotions are calm and content in your rucksack. If they were inside you they would still be calm," Leon replied.

"It's a beautiful feeling. I want to stay in this place away from all my troubles at home forever." Ruby decided.

"You can stay in this place and be where ever you want including home. Once you embrace the learning of the fear trap you can choose your state Ruby where ever you are."

"Please keep going Leon. Please tell me about this place called Anatonia" Ruby sat up in her seat awaiting the next instalment.

Leon was pleased to see Ruby looking so relaxed and confident. He continued.

I slept for over ten hours, a light sleep, full of dreams and memories of everything I had experienced over the last few days. Even though my mind was ticking over I was still relaxed and still looking forward to seeing Anatonia. The land of dreams.

I made breakfast and sat up on a chair in the cabin. It was 8.30 am, I took out the lover's card from my top pocket and studied it. It had a picture of a male and female holding hands. The male was looking at the female and the female was looking up to a beautiful light in the sky, the backdrop was a calm blue sea lit up by a sunset. It reminded me of Osclouro's sculpture on the cave wall.

The female and male figures were both naked and covered in flowers and gold leaves. The whole picture blended beauty, love and peace. I felt grounded after my conversations with the magician and violinist. Maybe Anatonia is where I will discover calm and peace.

"Earth and Water" Ruby interrupted.

"Yes Ruby, I was beginning to understand that I was already experiencing the learnings of Osclouro. My meeting with the Magician and Violinist was the introduction of my grounding journey."

"And Anatonia, was going to provide you with the calm and relaxation part" Ruby said excitedly.

"Yes Ruby, oh and so much more. My life was about to completely change," Leon smiled.

Around midday the boat started to drift to the side of the water's edge and slowly chugged along until it found a place to moor. I had stayed in the cabin as I had felt uncomfortable stepping outside and seeing water. After feeling so good, I didn't want to put an unnecessary risk on myself.

A few minutes after the boat had stopped and shut of its engine I packed a bag and stepped outside the cabin. It was so bright outside I could not open my eyes. The sun was beating down from a clear sky. It was hot and sunny in Anatonia.

As my vision cleared, I could make out young men and women running towards my boat, calling out in welcoming excited voices.

I was taken back by their beauty. The young ladies were all dressed in short grass skirts and bikini tops with long blonde hair and toned curved bodies. The guys had tanned skin, athletic bodies and short dark hair. They were all of similar heights and builds with perfect features and smiling faces.

I could not take my eyes off the young ladies faces. They were so beautiful.

"Hi there, come ashore," they all screamed excitedly.

I carefully disembarked, immediately the young girls grabbed my hand and led me to their town, which was nestled in the palm trees at the edge of the clear lake. As I walked rose petals were thrown over me like confetti and sweet fruit punch was served to me in coconut shells. This was paradise.

The town was even more magnificent. They lived in tree houses, which were connected by rope ladders, waterfalls gushed sparkling water into the lakes and warm sand tickled the feet. The bright sun lit the town in an incredible rainbow of colours, there were flowers and fruit trees everywhere. The people of Anatonia glided round in an elegant and childlike way and meditated every day.

"I had heard the saying, love was in their air, but in Anatonia it really was in the air" Leon reminisced.

"Anatonia sounds like the place of dreams" Ruby said, "Were there any older people or children?"

"There were only young adults Ruby."

"So where were all the families, children and older people?" Ruby asked confused.

"People came to Anatonia to discover true love. Once they found it they moved away to enjoy their love away from Anatonia. They saw it as their life purpose to promote love around the world. If they fell in love with each other, sometimes they would go away on their journey together.

"And what happens if they didn't manage to discover true love?" Ruby asked sadly.

Leon sensed that Ruby was bringing up her own issues.

"They always did. Some left after only six months and some left after ten years. Sometimes they left as a heterosexual couple, sometimes they left as a same sex couple and sometimes they just left on their own, having learnt the true meaning of love. It did not matter, there were no judgements of how love was discovered."

"You see Ruby, sometimes people confuse love with our world of modern relationships with all the pressure and expectation that goes with it. Chasing a romance that most of the time ends in stress, disappointment and then divorce. True love doesn't just come and go dependant on the pressures of the world and how people feel at the time"

"And of course then there is sex?" Leon added.

Ruby blushed. She was not ready to talk to Leon about her sexual issues. In fact she was not ready to talk to anybody.

Leon had recognised immediately that he was entering a sensitive subject.

"The attitude to sex in Anatonia was like nothing I had ever experienced before" Leon continued. "They simply saw sexual contact as a wonderful act of creation. The creation of positive energy, fun, increased love and new life. They talked about it freely and flirted with one another without jealously and guilt."

"Once they found their true love they then reserved their sexual energy for each other, so in partnership they could create great things together."

"There was no mindless bragging, no comparisons or judgements and no embarrassment, in fact they seemed to be flaunting their sexual energy all the time" Leon added.

"Were you turned on Leon?" Ruby asked unexpectedly.

Leon smiled.

"Ruby, I had spent the last ten years of my life sexually dead. My relationship with my last girlfriend ended in disaster. I lost all confidence in myself and my sex drive was zero. I had given up.

In Anatonia, from the minute I stepped off the boat, feelings of sexual excitement flooded my whole body. My fears disappeared and I just wanted to hug every girl and kiss them all over."

"And did you?" Ruby asked.

Leon looked straight into Ruby's eyes. He could see her past suffering, he could see her sexual energy completely suffocated by stress and fear.

"If I told you would you get turned on Ruby?" Leon asked.

Ruby shrunk back into her chair uncomfortable.

"I'm not even sure what that feels like anymore," Ruby muttered to herself.

Leon picked up the light off the bar and placed it into Ruby's hand.

"Ruby pretend this light is magic, pretend it takes away all your fears, worries and regrets. Pretend you no longer care about anything apart from experiencing loving energy. Forget the past and forget the future. Just be mindful of the now and let the feelings flow in without fear. Trust me, accept all the sensations and let yourself float, as if in a dream."

Ruby held onto the light and immediately felt a sense of calm. Leon seemed to understand the tension she was carrying and made issues around this normally embarrassing subject somehow feel very normal.

"I spent many days in the town living with the people from Anatonia. Many of the blond girls flirted with me, I think the fact that I was old and out of shape somehow made me different, a bit of a novelty I suppose. I grew at peace with myself and walked around bare-chested and full of confidence. I spent my days working in the fields and my nights dancing and socialising. I felt like I was in heaven.

One girl in particular used to sit with me and stroke my hair at night, she would cuddle up to me pushing her breasts against me. She often looked up and stared into my eyes, making me feel totally relaxed and dreamy before she would kiss me passionately. I observed her flirting with other men and women in the town. She would have been referred to as easy or loose in our modern day world, but in Anatonia she was seen as very beautiful with the gift of exceptional sexual energy."

"Is this the girl you found true love with?" Ruby asked.

"No Ruby, I was not looking for true love. I just wanted to experience the feelings I thought I would never experience again, and I did every single day, not just in sexual encounters with others, but also the feeling of being alive again. I felt love in me just walking in the fields to work in the morning. I also started to love the world again" Leon replied.

"Why did you leave Anatonia? If you hadn't found true love?" Ruby asked.

"I never said I didn't find true love, I said I wasn't looking for it" Leon leant forward and raised his eyebrows.

"You did find love?" Ruby she took a long sip of her drink.

"I decided to venture to the rock pools. A good friend had told me that this was a beautiful place with rare fish and sea-creatures on the far side of the plantation. It was a very hot day, not one cloud in the sky, so I waited until the afternoon when it was a bit cooler to take a stroll over.

I was not disappointed, it was a beautiful place. There were sparkling waterfalls against a backdrop of rose bushes and white towering rocks. The rock pools were full of colourful fish gliding through the clear water like streams of velvet.

As I explored the pools, I became aware of somebody hiding in the trees. I called out a welcoming hello, but they seem to retreat back into the bushes. I carried on walking around the rocks and gazing into the beautiful pools.

I reached one of the large pools towards the centre and knelt down to observe the wildlife.

"Beautiful isn't it"

The soft voice from behind startled me and I spun round to find a young girl crouching down behind me.

She was different from the girls I had seen here, her hair and features were darker, her frame was smaller and she had a shyness about her that was rarely seen in Anatonia.

"Yes, very beautiful" I replied.

"Where are you from?" She asked.

"Uhm. From a long way away" I replied, struggling to find the right answer.

"Oh," she replied and then she immediately jumped up and danced off towards the trees.

I shouted for her name, but it was no good she had disappeared.

Each day after work I returned to the rock pools. I came back because I wanted to see this young girl again, but after several weeks of visits she did not appear.

Life in Anatonia somehow started to become different for me. I started to feel uneasy and sad that I may not see this young girl again. The thought of the return of the awful days of anxiety and depression was playing on my mind, but I put in place everything that Fergus had told me and this made me feel better.

On one very hot day I managed to find a shady spot under a palm tree at the edge of one the rock pools. The water made me feel anxious, I had to move back so I could not see the edge.

"What's wrong?"

The soft voice returned. I looked round to see the beautiful young girl crouching to the side of me.

"Where did you come from?" I asked

"You seem troubled?" She said.

"Yes. I am not feeling well. It's nothing" I replied.

"My name is Luca. Is there anything I can do to help you?" She smiled.

"No I'm fine really. My name is Leon. It's lovely to meet you." I forced a smile back.

"Are you afraid of water?" Luca asked.

"Well yes I am. Why do you ask?" I replied.

"I have watched you over the past weeks. You visit the pools, but never bathe in the water. Even on scorching hot days? What are you afraid of? Some of them are very shallow" Luca enquired.

"Uhm, I guess it is what you call a phobia. I fear water" I shrugged.

Luca walked slowly towards one of the rock pools and peered in.

"One of the most curious creatures in these pools is the sun shrimp. It spends its days gliding across the water looking for patches of sunlight. When it senses danger it curls into a little ball, and produces prickles all over its skin to stop anything getting close to it, hiding its pink soft belly.

The sun shrimp has this automatic fear response to keep itself safe. The problem is it triggers this response whenever it meets another creature and so lives alone in constant fear of the next perceived danger. Despite it feeling desperate and lonely it pushes everything away, it doesn't let anything in. Even things that could help it.

Leon. Can you trust me?" Luca looked directly into my eyes.

"Well I don't really know you"

"Is there a part of you that trusts me Leon?" Luca repeated softly.

"Yes. I guess there is a part of me that does," I replied.

"Leon. Ask that part to meet me here tonight at midnight. I shall be waiting."

Luca jumped up and danced into the trees. She was out of sight in seconds.

That night I left my tree house just before midnight and made my way to the rock pools carrying a flame torch.

I arrived at the pool just past midnight and sat in the same place under the palm tree.

"Hiya Leon" Luca's soft voice whispered in my ear.

She seemed to appear from nowhere.

I could make out the features of Luca in the flickering light. She looked even more beautiful. Her hair was tied back, she had ringlets hanging down over her forehead. She wore a pretty white dress, perfectly shaped around her body and had an aura of sweet roses.

"Wow, you are beautiful" I said.

"Thank you, so are you. Follow me" Luca took my hand and led me through the trees.

The sky was full of shining stars, the midnight air was warm. It was silent apart from the sounds of our footsteps moving through the trees. In the distance I could hear the gentle waves lapping against the shore.

Luca turned and smiled and then led me through the final set of palm trees onto a small white sandy beach, only a few steps away from the water's edge. I looked out to sea and could see nothing but open water leading to the horizon. My fear returned in an instant.

"I must go back" I said.

"Leon, look into my eyes" Luca said quickly.

"As I looked into her eyes, something happened to me. A new thought entered my head. There is something I need to learn here!"

"Leon, breathe slowly and then copy me" Luca said calmly.

She took one sharp breath in and then held in for a second, before releasing the air slowly. As she breathed out she made a Ha sound. Once all the air was released, she held her position again for a second before she repeated the inward breath.

"Leon breathe in through your nose for three or four seconds, hold it for a second and then breathe out slowly through your mouth for six or seven seconds, hold it and then repeat again. On the outward breath make the Ha sound."

I tried it a few times until it became comfortable.

"Now breathe from your diaphragm, as you breathe in push your stomach out and as you breathe out and release the air pull back your stomach in."

We continued to breathe together in this way for a few minutes.

"Now look out to the horizon and find a star in the sky" Luca pointed.

I noticed a small bright star in the sky directly ahead and above and concentrated my attention on this.

"Keep doing that, and bring your attention down to the top of the water, so both the water and the star is in view, keeping your head still" Luca continued.

Luca then moved to the side of me and walked along the beach.

"Now keeping your head still Leon, bring me into your vision"

I was now staring at the star, the water and the beautiful figure of Luca on the beach"

"Now visualise my image on the opposite side of the beach, as if I'm looking at a reflection of myself. Leon relax and be still and just focus on the four images."

I felt dreamy, I was distracted momentarily from my fear as my vision extended outwards, I continued to Ha breathe as Luca's voice continued softly.

"Leon now imagine you can see the beautiful palm trees behind, extend your vision three hundred and sixty degrees, relax your body and breathe."

"Breathe energy in, see with clarity, breathe out and drop your shoulders and totally relax, accepting any sensations into the process. All sensations are now good sensations. Trust me. This is the secret behind creating human energy passed down from generation to generation through the brave monks of Eth."

I stayed there for several minutes. I had never felt like this before and it was beautiful.

Luca took my hand and led to me towards the water.

My concentration broke as fear smothered me.

Luca stopped, "It's OK, just breathe and go back into your peripheral vision. Please just trust me Leon." She squeezed my hand to reassure me.

I refocused and slowly we walked towards the water's edge.

"Reconnect to the beauty of your inner soul Leon, where love and compassion waits patiently for you. Unveil the part of you that loves you"

"I can't do that, my fear won't let me. This part of me is filled with darkness not love Luca. You don't understand"

Luca smiled and leant towards me, she kissed me on the lips. Her soft lips talked to me, it will be alright.

"I'm looking forward to walking into the darkness with you," she kissed me again and led me into the water.

As the water washed around my feet, the sensations of fear hit me hard.

Intense butterflies fluttered around inside and my head became heavy and tense. My heart started pumping, I had chest pains and I came over dizzy, feint and sick. That awful feeling of derealisation retuned.

"What colour are your butterflies?" Luca asked.

"What do you mean?"

"What colour are they, the butterflies inside you?"

"I don't know" I replied confused.

"I know you don't, but if you did what colour would they be"

"Black" I answered without thinking.

"What shape are they" Luca continued.

"I really don't know Luca. What do you mean?"

"Leon please trust me, stop thinking and just answer. First thing that comes into your head?" Luca smiled.

"OK, square" I replied.

"Are they three dimensional or flat?"

"Three dimensional" I replied

"Are they moving or still?"

"Moving"

"Fast or slow"

"They are moving fast"

"Big or small?"

"They are medium sized" I was just answering without thinking now.

"Heavy or light?"

"Heavy" I said.

"What noise are they making?"

"A horrible roaring sound that gets louder and louder as they speed up"

"Leon. Turn them light yellow and make them round" Luca said suddenly.

"What?" I said confused.

"Just go with it Leon" Luca assured me again.

"Now make the yellow circles lighter"

"OK Luca." I said visualising the change inside of me.

"Make them flat, two dimensional"

"OK"

"Now slow them down and start to make them smaller. As they shrink, play the roaring sound back to yourself, but this time play it backwards, so it starts loud and then goes quieter and quieter. Make the sound Leon"

"It sounds funny" I replied starting to laugh.

"Now slow them down until they stop and are now tiny dots."

"I visualised these tiny yellow dots, flat, still and quiet"

"Now take these tickle bumps with you with all your love and care" Luca said playfully, before leading me deeper into the sea.

The sensations felt different inside of me, it was peaceful.

The water was now up to my waist. My head and heart was pounding, I had to stop.

"Please. We must stop now" I said to Luca turning around.

"Your heavy head, sickness, fuzziness and pounding heart is the same feel we have when falling in love, true love when nothing else matters. Withdraw from your body and float into love with me Leon." Luca kissed the back of my neck.

I turned around and amongst all the awful thoughts, a new thought popped into my head.

I have never died from fear, I've never died from the sensations of fear. What if these sensations are trying to actually trying to lead me somewhere? To this place of love that Luca is suggesting.

"Do not dwell on the nasty thoughts Leon. They are just thoughts, we all have them they are not important. Just act on the nice thoughts, they will show the way to love" Luca smiled.

"Leon, dance with the sensations; don't fight them. Dance."

We walked deeper into the water. I walked into the storm, faced and floated into my fears. Right here is where I found the true meaning of acceptance.

My sensations dissolved, I felt nothing but a huge blanket of peace.

Tears rolled down my face. I had found paradise.

"It's not our experiences that define us. It's how we learn to experience our experiences that defines us. You no longer need to retreat Leon." Luca was the most beautiful person I had ever met.

That night, Luca and I made love in the water. I had found real love for the first time. Not only in another person, but also in myself. Fear had been replaced with love.

In our final embrace, Luca started to feel different, she moved away and smiled at me one last time. Somehow I knew she was different. Somehow I had guessed. Her body was changing.

Ruby thought about herself. Could this really happen for me?

"Yes Ruby it can. It's just a matter of searching inside and unveiling what was always there. It's at the core of all of us. Innate love, before all the stuff in life clouded the waters" Leon answered.

Luca whispered her final goodbyes, dived into the water and swam away, her huge golden tail shimmering like a thousand diamonds in the sunset.

Ruby decided to hug Leon. They held each other tightly. Everything just seemed to feel right.

The scene at the bar had moved on. The tall lady had retired for the day. The bare-chested man was slumped over the bar snoring. The round creature was crunching on a bowl of nuts. The barman was setting up a tables on the beach ready for the evening guests.

"What an amazing story. You found the answer, Earth, the grounding knowledge you received from the magician and violinist. Water, Peace and Love from Luca. Air, the Monks of Eth breathing that creates wonderful energy and Fire. I guess this is the power and purpose to move forward and help people, no matter what?" Ruby asked.

"Yes Ruby, the same story that Osclouro taught his apprentices. I returned home with the story that you must now embrace yourself and live yourself and teach to others who are experiencing their own anxieties. No matter what state they have got into." Leon nodded over at the man slumped over the bar.

"Some people hold onto their issues you know Ruby. It provides them with something, a secondary gain sat in their deeper thinking. It defines them in some way, so they decide to hold on to their anxiety. Many times they are not aware they are doing it. By creating curiosity and desire to change the fear trap is eventually released."

"Ruby nodded. I will help as many people as possible Leon. I have a lot of making up to do" Ruby peered down at her bag lying there completely still and at peace.

Leon smiled. "I have to go now Ruby. There is still one more thing I have to do."

"Oh please don't leave Leon. Can this thing not wait?"

"Ruby, remember what Fergus said to me. If I hadn't visited Eth Street then I hadn't lived. The final I thing I had to face to completely break the fear trap" Leon pulled out a card out of his top pocket and placed in onto the bar.

Ruby looked down and saw a picture of a fire breathing dragon in front of an old dark castle. There were no words.

"I have to go now Ruby"

"Don't leave me Leon. Can I come with you?"

Leon turned and smiled, "You are always with me Ruby. You are never alone. Think back. How did you get here? How did you get on this beach?"

As Leon was talking, the scene starting to slowly fade away. Everything was going blurry. Ruby was struggling to make out the image of Leon in front of her.

"Remember Ruby, I am with you everywhere you go."

Leon's voice was now just a whisper and Ruby was in total darkness.

Ruby jolted up in bed. The morning light was breaking through the crack in the curtains. Her alarm clock was flashing 6.00am. She was back in her bedroom, back in London.

9 A NEW ACQUAINTANCE

That morning everything had felt totally different. Ruby had skipped to work. The scenery looked brighter even though nothing had changed. Ruby had even spent time putting on her most expensive make-up and styled her hair. Ringlets included.

She felt and looked great.

As she arranged the flowers in the shop, she admired the natural beauty of each flower and took a moment to appreciate each of their wonderful scents.

Her manager Victoria couldn't help notice the transformation and found the right moment to ask her what was happening?

"I had a dream Victoria, the most amazing dream last night. I felt I was really there. I mean I was there. Thinking, talking and feeling. It was honest and real and seemed to unlock the truth about life."

Victoria stood still. Mouth wide open.

"You see Victoria. Things all of sudden seem different. Somewhat simpler. I have decided to live my life and be happy and help as many people as I can people to be happy."

"What about your anxiety Ruby?" Victoria had to ask.

"I don't care if it's there or not. I will live life how I want to live it and do things I want to do. If I don't panic, then that's fine. If I do panic, then that's fine too. I will handle it. Starting with phoning my sister. I am going to be walking down the aisle with her carrying the most beautiful flower arrangement ever created."

Victoria smiled at Ruby and found an excuse to nip under the counter. She shed a happy tear.

After telling her sister the good news, Ruby decided to have lunch in a French patisserie overlooking the park. She has always wanted to go there, but in the past had felt way too uncomfortable.

As she sipped her freshly squeezed orange juice, she recalled her dream piece by piece. I wish I could go back and see my friend Leon again.

A handsome middle aged gentleman interrupted her thoughts. "I'm sorry to bother you, may I sit here?"

The patisserie was busy and people were beginning to share tables.

"Of course" Ruby replied.

In the past Ruby would have dreaded this kind of encounter and dropped her head to avoid any eye contact or embarrassing small talk.

After a few minutes Ruby plucked up the courage to ask something.

"Do you work around here?"

"Yes, just around the corner. I run a solicitors office and you?"

"I work in the flower shop just a few streets away by the station" Ruby replied.

"It must be much more fun giving flowers than arranging expensive legal agreements. Have you got any jobs available?"

"I could train you if are happy to take the salary drop. My name is Ruby by the way, what's your name?"

"Tom. To be honest Ruby I've had a terrible morning, everything has gone wrong at work today, I've lost a fortune. Even more than my divorce cost me. So I decided to take a break over here."

"Well its only money Tom. I'm sure you will have a great day tomorrow."

"Are you always this happy Ruby?"

Ruby laughed. If only you knew what my life has been like.

"No not always. I just got up in a good mood this morning" Ruby replied.

"What, nice dreams?" Tom said.

"Yes. An amazing dream. I actually felt I was really there. Do you know what I mean?"

"I dreamt like that when I was kid" Tom said.

"I guess my dreams have now been replaced by reality. Anyway back to the grindstone" Tom added.

"I guess my reality has now been replaced by dreams" Ruby smiled.

"Are you married or do you have a boyfriend"

"No. I just have a loving cat"

"I know we have just met, but there's something about you Ruby. You are different from the people I normally spend my days with. Would you consider coming out with me for a drink one night" Tom said.

"Yes, I would love to Tom" Ruby replied. Where was this coming from?

Tom typed Ruby's number into his phone and arranged to pick her up on Friday night.

"Oh by the way Ruby. You should pop into Sifu Ku Wong's studio after work. I have started kung fu lessons with him. He is always talking about waking up in dreams and things like that" Tom left in happiness.

After work Ruby carried on her normal nighty routine, walked home, fed and cuddled her cat and put her feet up in front of the television, but this time knowing she had a date for the first time in years.

She then had a sudden urge to go out. I want to go and see this kung fu master. Maybe I can catch him after his lesson and ask him about my dream.

Sifu Ku Wong's studio was found up a staircase at the side of a betting shop. A large golden dragon statue invited his students into an open room with matted floor.

When Ruby arrived a small group were just leaving with their gym bags. Sifu Ku Wong was a small Chinese man, probably in his seventies. He was sitting at a desk in the corner still in his white robes.

"Hello, young lady" Sifu called over.

"Hi" Ruby walked over and took a seat.

"You like to join our class?" Sifu asked, pushing a registration form over the desk.

"Thanks. Maybe one day, but could I ask you something first? I know it may sound strange but I bumped into one of your students who said you may be able to help me with a dream I had?"

Sifu laughed. "I have many people ask for help, but not often about dreams? Only you can interpret your own dreams."

"Well it was the fact that the dream felt so real. It has changed me in every way. I feel totally different about life. I am acting different. In the dream, objects were solid, I could gather thoughts and speak my views. It was the same as real life" Ruby felt strange saying what she was saying to a complete stranger.

"I see" Sifu said.

The last of his students left the room.

"I feel a bit stupid for mentioning it. I'm sorry. Yes, I would like to register for a class and then I must be getting home." Ruby thought the distraction of registering for the programme would curb her embarrassment and cause a distraction.

"Thank you. I see you every Friday night at 7.00pm. I am strict about kung fu practice. It's only way to learn. So you must be here on time. No excuses"

"OK thank you" Ruby replied as she stood up to leave. What have I got myself into now?

Ruby walked away and opened the door to leave,

"Did you have outstanding task in your dream?" Sifu said as Ruby had just passed through the doorway.

"I'm sorry" Ruby peered back around the door.

"Did you or any of your dream characters have outstanding task?"

"Yes. Yes they did" Ruby quickly made her way back and sat back down. "A man called Leon, he had to go to some road called Eth Street otherwise he would not have lived or something like that."

"Did you say Eth Street" Sifu asked leaning forward.

"Yes I think so. No I'm absolutely sure Eth Street it was"

Sifu leant back in his chair and stroked his chin. There was a period of silence.

"You must return Ruby. I must help you go back."

10 THE FEAR TRAP

"Go back. How? Why?" Ruby said in astonishment.

"Sit down and relax Ruby, I have something to show you"

Sifu leant down and shuffled around in his draw for a few moments before producing a parchment rolled up in a leather tube.

He placed the parchment carefully onto his desk and asked Ruby to read it.

Ruby looked down at the title; *the village of Eth*.

It read;

A long time ago, a peaceful race of human beings lived in a beautiful tribal village.

The village was simple in design. The people lived in hand made huts, cooked food on open fires and washed their clothes in the nearby streams.

During the days, the villagers went about their lives in a productive and happy way.

They fished the rivers, grew their food and made items of clothing, furniture and gifts with natural elements that surrounded them.

The village was self-sufficient. Everybody contributed to provide what it needed to maintain the health and harmony of its people.

There was no organised hierarchy and no elected leaders. The villagers had equal respect for one another. The older members were looked after by everybody in the village. They were seen as wise and precious. They would be called upon to help solve any challenges that the village faced, facilitate any disputes and teach and nurture anybody who required help. They also passed down the spiritual teachings from generation to generation.

As part of their spiritual culture, the villagers believed everybody had a unique positive innate purpose for entering this lifetime. They supported each other to flourish in their chosen path in any way possible.

The fishermen would become masters of their trade, the gardeners would grow the freshest and tastiest vegetables, craftsman would produce amazing products and doctors would search for the best remedies. All the men and women chose their areas of interest and all enjoyed each and every day doing what they loved.

After the busy days, the villagers congregated around the campfires to sing, dance and feast. The children would enjoy putting on shows they had practiced during the day; the wise men would hold spiritual relaxation sessions and the villagers took it in turns to organise games and entertainment.

A day of treats and gifts was organised for people celebrating their birthdays. Marriages and births were celebrated in style; death was seen as a celebration of life and the passing over to the next stage of life.

There was no money, no sin, no judgements and no competition between each other.

Progression was seen as mastering your own trade and helping others mastering theirs. Gaining a greater spiritual understanding and growing love and happiness was seen as true progression and development.

The villagers were healthy and relaxed. They were not driven by fear, guilt, anger or sadness. These emotions were not part of their culture. Stress, anxiety and depression had not been invented.

They managed their challenges as a group, sticking together and helping each other through the tough times.

The wise men and women, through their spiritual teachings, would teach the tribe to enter an incredible dream world whilst they were sleeping. This dream world could either be accessed through deep meditation or during light sleep. It was believed that events experienced in the dream world manifested in the real world. It was a hugely powerful part of their existence.

As the villagers became more connected with their spiritual minds, they could enter the dream world each time they slept. Here, they were able to experience a magical life controlled through their thoughts whilst their body remained rested in sleep.

The villagers entered this world to find answers to any questions that they could not solve on the physical plain. They also navigated the world to find inner peace, strength and deeper happiness that they brought into their mind and body in the waking world.

It was said that the most advanced spiritual wise people were able to connect to the source of life itself and would live in both the awake and sleep world as one powerful being in a continued state of pure bliss. Legend had it that on the first day of each season change they would meet up in dream world in a magical cave nestled in a beautiful wood. Here they would join together and become one Supreme Being. It was this connection to the oneness that brought peace to their people, dissolving any of the unimportant worries that the village may have.

Ultimately, they all lived a happy and content life in beautiful natural surroundings.

One day a stranger called Rulo arrived at the village, he looked different to the tribal people. His skin was pale, he talked in a foreign language and he dressed in tailored clothes. He asked for food and water and a place to rest overnight. The tribe looked after the man and treated him to the splendours of the village.

He stayed for several nights and when he left gave the eldest tribeswoman a handful of silver coins. Not understanding the concept of money, the tribe accepted the odd silver round objects as a gift and proudly displayed them on a post in the village.

The stranger then invited one of the tribe to join him on his travels to learn from other civilisations and bring back the knowledge to the village. A young wise women called Soco who had fallen in love with the pale-faced traveller agreed to the offer and they both left with a wonderful send-off party.

On the night of the party, the oldest man in the village invited the two lovers into his tent. He was frail. Confined to his bed, he had not left his tent for the past year and it was now only a matter of hours before he was ready to pass over to the next world.

His tent was basic, dimly lit by scented candles place on a rickety bedside cabinet. The scent was sweet, the atmosphere had a feeling of warmth and calm.

He asked Soco to retrieve a small wooden box from under his bed and carefully passed a small key to Rulo from under his pillow. He then instructed the couple to open the box and take out the contents.

Soco placed the contents wrapped in a handkerchief on the bed beside the old man. He gestured to Rulo to unwrap the handkerchief whilst sitting back in his bed with his eyes closed.

Rulo gently unwrapped the package and placed it on the bed. Soco and Rulo held hands as they studied the set of wooden picture cards. Each card carefully carved in bright colours, depicting scenes of magical creatures, stunning landscapes and beautiful smiling figures. The words on the cards were jumbled, anagrams hiding secret messages.

The old man muttered his final words. "Take these on your journey, bathe in the wisdom of the cards and return with your love." He was then silent.

The Fear Trap

Soco pulled a sheet over the old man's man face, knelt down and preyed through her soft tears. The loving couple paid their final regards, mounted their horses and rode off into the sunset.

Several months later, a large group of pale-faced men turned up at the village. This time they did not ask to stay, they announced that all the land was now under ownership of a governor of the region and that he wanted to help the village build a system to benefit from the new arrangements.

He invited a group of the wisest women and men in the village to a private meeting and awarded them the title of the group leaders. For this honour he presented them with more silver coins and told them they had the responsibility for making the new system work for all the people in the village.

He announced that he would give all the tribespeople in the village silver coins in return for fish, vegetables, clothing and supplies. In return he would introduce brand new luxuries to the village and award them for carrying out their duties in line with their new special status.

The village worked hard to supply the additional provisions. Each day the group of pale-faced men would collect their goods and hand over more silver coins. Over time the wise men and women in the village began to communicate more clearly with the strangers. They were told that they would be able to use the coins to buy food and products from anywhere they wanted across the land. In exchange for some of the coins the eldest tribeswoman was presented with a beautiful gold necklace with the highest honour engraved in emeralds from one of the strangers.

She wore it with pride around the village, she had accepted it as a gift. The majority of tribespeople were happy for her. However, something unusual was beginning to happen. The fishermen were starting to complain that they had to work harder than the rest of village to produce the extra stocks. Some of food in the village was being rationed and a small number of tribespeople were questioning why the eldest tribeswoman had been given a gold necklace. A brand new emotion called jealously was born.

The wise men and women sensed the change in the fisherman and decided to invite the strangers to a village meeting to explain the new system and how the silver coins could bring the village new and wonderful luxuries. The pale-faced gentlemen listened to the concerns of the fisherman and then came up with a new solution. They suggested that the silver coins should be distributed directly to each tribesman based on the value of the service he or she provides. They could swap the coins between each other in exchange for their products or services.

The fisherman decided that this would be a fairer way and the wise men and women agreed to help set the values in the new system in an attempt to make the village happy again. As time passed, the medicine men and women and wise men and women started to collect most the coins and became rich, followed by the fisherman who also had many possessions. The rest of the village had enough coins to survive but became poorer and small charitable hand outs supported the lame and weak.

The village became used to this way of life, and accepted the system. The wise men and medicine men and women moved to larger huts at one end of the village close to the river. The fishermen became very competitive with each other in order to win more coins. The rest of the village started to become ill through lack of nourishing food and stress caused by their lack of money. A brand new competitive game was born.

The tribes no longer congregated at night time, the wise men and women sat together and the fishermen partied in their own small groups, most of the other villages stayed in their huts. Meditation and spiritual teachings were practised by the wise men, the rich and their families, but forgotten everywhere else.

The medicine men and women could not meet the demand, so they decided to increase their prices to reduce the time they had to work and receive more coins for their precious services.

There were instances where poor tribal members needed medicine or advice from the wise leaders, but just could not afford to pay the rates. Some of the villagers became angry and stole from the rich.

The wise men and women grew more concerned about the village, they had the responsibility to maintain their status in the system for the overall good of the village, so decided to write up a set of rules. Any of the tribespeople that broke the new rules would be punished. The rich tribal leaders paid a group of the strongest members in the village to police the new system and things settled down again for a while.

The wise men and women also became competitive with each other, as the huts got bigger and the possessions increased. They set up more complex value systems and tried to win silver coins off each other through their knowledge of the system. Some of the wise people became anxious and stressed as they started to lose the silver coin battle. Some of the weaker fishermen fell into poverty and became depressed and ill. The winners of the system enjoyed their enormous wealth, but were always worried that it would be taken from them and were always on their guard. They trusted nobody.

The young adults in the village would put pressure on themselves to attract the most successful men and women. They would be desperate to be the most popular, the most intelligent the strongest in the group. Families would put pressure on each other to maintain their status in the system.

Their appearance was now critical to attract the right partner and ensure they met the expectations of the parents and their peers. They would put themselves under enormous pressure to lose weight and stay looking young. The pressure often resulted in the opposite result and overeating became a common challenge.

The village carried on for several more years, crimes were committed, punishment was administered and silver coins became the new spiritual worship for all tribesmen rich or poor. The rich had all kinds of new exciting items brought to them from across the land.

Although the system did not seem fair, it did hold the village together in some kind of order and many of the villagers had forgotten what is used to be like.

One day, five years later, the two travellers returned to the village. They were shocked at the changes they saw. They experienced anger, sadness, guilt and an enormous sense of mistrust and fear. The pale-faced traveller blamed himself for the demise of the village and the simple life he had fallen in love with during his short visit. He demanded that it returned back to how it was. However the rich were too fearful to go backwards and lose everything they had worked for and the poor were busy making the system work for them.

His travelling companion Soco was now his wife and carrying their baby. They had returned to the village to settle down as a family. She was more considered in her approach.

She looked into the eyes of the villagers both rich and poor and realised that something had changed at a deeper level. Something this new human race would not be able to reverse.

This was just a stage in the evolution of the human race and there would be more challenges to come.

This next stage of the cycle had begun and the ancient spiritual secrets must now be protected to help this new race find peace in their new world. She felt compassion for both the rich and the poor, there was the same look of fear in their eyes.

She then turned to her husband and reminded him of some of the most secret spiritual teachings they had shared on their travels. They took a step back, hugged, held hands and took a slow deep breath. We will help everybody; nobody will be excluded. It is time to break out of the fear trap.

Ruby rolled up the parchment carefully and handed it back to Sifu.

She then sat for a minute in silence. Everybody must be feeling the pressure. She was still trying to link up the reason for her particular dream and why she needed to now go back.

"Why me?" Ruby asked.

"By going back you will help break the fear trap for many more people" Sifu replied.

"How I can help people. I have trouble just coping with myself" Ruby protested.

"If you think you are too small to make an impact, try going to bed with mosquito" Sifu smiled.

"How do you know about all this?" Ruby asked

"I have also been on journey. I now spend my life building energy in people so they can experience a spiritual, healthy and purposeful life. Now listen to me carefully, I need you follow my instructions every night until you find way back into your dream. You need to find the waking dream state again."

"Maybe I should give up my possessions, my flat in London and help people who have fallen off their path," Ruby suggested.

"Remember what Soco said, what we see today is just a stage in the evolution of our people. You can continue to prosper in this world, you do not need to give away your possessions. It is how you view the world and contribute as you go that defines how you can help people around you," Sifu replied.

Ruby took a breath and pondered over Sifu's words.

"I understand and I'm ready to go back and complete my learning Sifu," Ruby said confidently.

"Good. Before we start, these cards in your dreams, the musician, the lovers and the dragon. They are from sacred deck of cards carved in the village all those years ago. Some of words in your dream will be jumbled. There are hidden messages everywhere Ruby."

"What do you mean, I don't know of any such words Sifu?"

"Well start with Eth Street. Try and rearrange words." Sifu replied.

"Eth Street" Ruby pondered.

"E T H, can be arranged to the T H E. I guess"

"Good Ruby, It's that's simple"

"S T R E E T could be T R E E T S, no that's not right" Ruby grabbed a pen and wrote the letters down.

"S T R E E T. Backwards that would be T E E R T S."

"So ok what about T E S E R T"

"I have it. T E S T E R"

"Eth Street is translated into The Tester"

"Well done Ruby. You must go back and find the tester," Sifu nodded.

The next few hours were spent learning bed time rituals and writing down everything Ruby could remember about her dream.

It was just before midnight when Ruby eventually got home. She was filled with excitement. The sensations that once caused her terror were now bursting with adrenaline fuelled curiosity. Her tension was the same, her thinking was now very different.

She tucked under the sheets with her cat curled up at the bottom of the bed and started what would now be her nightly ritual.

Every night she repeated Sifu's instructions. On the fourth night it happened again.

11 CITY OF ETH

A large Viking vessel sailed towards the harbour. Ruby stood on the deck with a diverse array of creatures. The captain of the ship, announced the destination through a loud speaker. They had arrived at the city of Eth.

Ruby looked up to see a busy port. Traders were swapping goods on small wooden boats. Viking ships were moored to the side. There were hundreds of crates floating in the sea and fishermen were shouting and gesturing to each other.

Reaching into the sky were two mountain peaks, a large monastery sat on the right and an old castle was perched on the higher peak to the left.

Ruby disembarked and observed her surroundings. The city was bustling. I know I'm dreaming. I need to stay asleep until I find the last piece of this story. How would I find Leon in such a busy place?

Ruby flagged down a horse and cart and asked the driver if he could take her to Eth Street. The old driver laughed "you need a different kind of transport to go there luv" as he pointed towards the old castle at the top of the mountain.

"How would I get there?" Ruby asked.

"You'll need to find a dragon I reckon" the old man shouted back as he carried on up the road.

OK, so I am definitely in dream world that's for sure. Ruby carried on walking until she arrived in a large square in the centre of a busy market place. There must be a way to the castle, I just need to find somebody to take me there.

In one corner of the square Ruby noticed a taxi rank. She headed over to a group of drivers huddled around a card table and asked for a ride. One driver offered to take her as far as the dragon sanctuary at the bottom of the mountain. Here she would find the dragon trainer who may possibly be able to help her.

The ride to the foot of the mountain was pleasantly smooth. The horse and cart seemed to leave the busy city quickly and Ruby was treated to scenery of rolling hills and open roads. As they approached the dragon sanctuary, Ruby could hear the sound of short bursts of raging fire. That must be the dragons she thought.

Ruby thanked the driver and handed over a gold piece she found in her pocket. The dragon sanctuary was accessed through a large wooden door between two large stone pillars. Inside there were huge cages with dragons sleeping peacefully inside. The stone cobbled floors were covered in pretty Persian rugs and the walls were scattered in paintings of dragon riding warriors.

"Hi Ruby. I am expecting you"

Ruby turned round and found to find a women dressed in silver armour. The sight of her incredible muscles and powerful frame made Ruby jump backwards.

"No need to be afraid Ruby. My name is Tala. I have been busily training your dragon for the past four days. She is a beauty. Come, come and see her. She is out in the training ground."

Ruby followed Tala outside to an open round field surrounded by the walls of the sanctuary. In the centre of the field the large red serpent like creature was sitting quietly. The dragon slowly blinked his golden-flecked emerald eyes

"Her name is Ruby also. She is strong, clever and kind. It's been a pleasure to train her. She will be more than capable of carrying you on your journey."

"Will she be taking me to the Castle?"

"Well, she will take you to the foot of Eth Street, from there you will on your own" Tala replied.

"Where is Eth Street?" Ruby asked.

"It's at the top of the mountain, and leads to the entrance of the dark castle where the tester spends his days," Tala replied.

"Why is the dark castle higher than the monastery? I would have thought it would have been the other way around, goodness over evil?"

"Well Ruby, the monastery does indeed represent relaxation, balance and contentment. The ancient monks of Eth teach these good virtues to the people. It is also recognised that when people push their boundaries and move away from their comfort zone then they will face fear. The dark castle represents this forward movement, which is why it sits higher. Being brave is not about getting rid of your fear; it is moving forward despite it. When you reach the top of the mountain the dark castle is not actually as scary as it seems. When you move out of your comfort zone, although uncomfortable at first, it soon gets comfortable again and the zone expands, which means you expand. In fact the castle and monastery merge into one sometimes."

"Who is the tester?" Ruby was curious and wanted to know as much as possible.

Tala looked up and smiled. "The tester is who you want it to be. The more you accept challenges and progress forward, the more he or she shows their face to test you."

"I don't like the sound of that" Ruby said.

"No Ruby it will be fine. The tester is actually there to help you drive forwards. He or she is there to help you. They arrive when things are tough to check if you're really serious about moving on."

"So does the tester create our fear" Ruby asked.

"Not always, but the tester will often throw in a fearful thought or two to test you. You then have the choice to acknowledge the thought and just let it go to act on the next happy thought that moves you forward. Or, you take on the thought as a problem and stay still."

"The more you get used to moving forward the more you get familiar with the tester. He or she then becomes another acquaintance. A tricky acquaintance mind you, but still very useful." Tala added.

Ruby had a sudden thought. If you haven't been to Eth Street you haven't lived.

"Will I have to face my tester Tala? I only came to find a friend of mine called Leon"

Tala laughed "Now you have come this far; surely you don't want to miss all the fun?"

Ruby smiled nervously. She knew deep down that soon she would be walking the path to the castle.

"Ruby, first you need to increase your fitness and energy. Do you know how to Ha breathe"

"Yes, Leon showed me how to do that." Ruby replied.

"Great. Ha breathing every day from now on. Also eat healthily and plenty of exercise. Not just here in your dreams Ruby, but when you return to your waking body."

"I have already joined a kung fu class" Ruby said proudly.

"Yes I know" Tala winked.

During the next few days Ruby and the dragon went through heavy training sessions. Tala also explained to Ruby that everybody has the life force of strength and beauty within themselves. This is the essence of the soul that sits in every living creature. All Ruby needed to do was to put her stuff to one side, get out of her own way and surrender to this beautiful power.

Ruby learnt how to ride on the dragon, how to control the direction by tapping on the side of her neck and how to signal to land by squeezing her arms tight around. Ruby was a beautiful creature. She moved with utmost grace, with sharp shiny ruby scales, strong leathery wings and a long snake like tongue.

Tala and Ruby shared many stories from their respective worlds and became very close friends. Ruby felt stronger and stronger. In dream world it took no time to get into fantastic physical shape. All the time Tala reminded Ruby how important it was to carry on this lifestyle in her waking world.

Ruby kept thinking, building up power and purpose. The fire element of the fear trap. The fitter I feel the better I feel.

Earth (Grounding), Water (Peace), Air (Breathing) and Fire (Power and Purpose). It all makes sense to me now.

On the third day, Ruby was woken by Tala. "It's time. Ruby is waiting outside to take you. Good luck!"

Ruby got her things together and walked out to the training ground. Her dragon was waiting patiently.

Ok here goes Ruby thought as she mounted the dragon.

"Thank you Tala. Will I see you again?" Ruby asked.

"I do hope so Ruby. You have been my favourite student. Remember Ruby, patience, persistence and perspiration make an unbeatable combination for success." Tala slapped the back of the dragon.

The dragon flapped its huge wings and launched into the air. Within a few seconds Tala and the dragon sanctuary were out of sight.

Fire raged out of the dragon's mouth as it flew towards the castle high up in the air. Power, Ruby thought. She was excited and nervous at the same time. The wind was blowing into her face and the energy was pouring through her body.

This is my chance to see Leon again and a chance to meet the tester. I have listened to all the wise words, I have a wonderful light inside me. I will no longer get in my own way and dwell on the past. I will no longer fight, I will dance!

I will follow Osclouro's wisdom, like hundreds and thousands of people before me. I will no longer live life through fear, I will experience life through love.

Just as Ruby's thoughts came to a natural conclusion, the dragon started to descend. It swooped downwards with its sleek swishing tail stretching up to the sky. In no time they reached the ground landing gracefully without a sound.

Ruby dismounted.

There was a narrow road winding up the hill, thick bushes and trees lined the edges. Ruby could make out the turrets of the dark castle ahead.

The dragon shuffled into launch position, slyly glaring at Ruby through the corner of her eye.

"Well here goes Ruby, save me some supper" Ruby said nervously.

The large creature disappeared into the distance; her roar echoed across the fields.

Ruby was now alone. It was silent.

12 A NEW BEGINNING

Ruby looked ahead towards the narrow winding path. Although she reminded herself this was just a dream, everything felt so real. The smells, the air, the images, an incredible feeling.

Ruby felt every sensation of fear inside her. She remembered her rucksack that had carried her emotions back at the beach bar. She knew she would carry her emotions as part of her from now on. That is what she wanted to feel the fear and just go for it; nothing could really hurt her anymore. Dance not fight, learn to love the world and not be angry with it.

She started to walk along the path, with each step she lifted her head higher, carried her body with purpose and breathed steadily. She was determined to do this, for herself.

It must have been twenty minutes before she noticed a figure peering out of the trees ahead. She slowed her steps and carried on forward maintaining her positive posture.

As she got closer the figure moved out from the trees and stood directly in front of her. He was tall and cloaked in dark robes. His old wrinkled face was mostly covered by a black velvet scarf. He was carrying a large leather book and was gesturing for Ruby to come closer.

Ruby continued with her steady breathing and adjusted her vision in the same way Leon had been taught by Luca the mermaid in Anatonia. She let the sensations of fear swirl around her body whilst maintaining her purposeful posture.

"Are you the tester?" she asked.

"You may think you are strong Ruby, but soon your panic and anxiety will reach a level you have never experienced before. Everything you have learnt has been another wasted effort, because you have something worse than anybody else. Your condition is different Ruby and you know it" The dark figure replied in a deep gruff voice.

"In the last few days, I have felt the happiest I've ever felt. I am filled with gratitude just for that. I will continue to surrender to what I've learnt. I will not fight anymore" Ruby replied.

"They are just words Ruby, you can pretend as long as you want, but you don't fool me and you cannot fool yourself. The darkness of anxiety will return and will get worse and you know it!"

"That's OK. I will continue to move forward and do what I can to help people in my world. One thing we all have is free will. I can choose to listen to you or I can choose to listen to somebody who is more chilled and more fun. Nobody is completely sure what they are doing here. Why don't you just lighten up a bit" Ruby smiled.

The dark figure took a step back, turned to the side and walked back into the woods.

Ruby was alone once more.

Ruby continued her journey along the winding path. Other than the odd sign nailed to the tree displaying the name Eth Street, the landscape remained consistent.

Finally a second figure appeared, looking similar to the first, dark robes and old features but slightly taller and definitely wider.

"So this is the sad woman called Ruby, dull, middle aged and all washed up. You may think you are brave now, but it is too late for you. Too old to enjoy life now; you have wasted your life." He pointed a large stick at Ruby as he spoke.

"We are all on a journey good man. Time is just a made up concept to get hung up about if you choose. I am only interested in now, in what I'm feeling now. I cannot do anything about yesterday and cannot know what tomorrow will bring. However, I can chose what I do now. I am compassionate, loving and kind to myself and others, because it makes me happy." Ruby was speaking with a growing confidence.

"You are in your forties, you have no children, you have no partner and you have done nothing with your life, you are just too old now to start a family. You are only fooling yourself. The truth is the truth" The dark man learnt forward and sneered.

Ruby took a step back and bowed her head. The comment about children had hit her hard. She closed her eyes and took four Ha breaths. Thoughts were racing into her head, awful thoughts, sad feelings rushed through her stomach.

Ruby then remembered the picture on the cave wall, the swirling lines always moving forward to the angel in the sky. I do not have to justify life to this man. All the things he talks about sit in the lower levels of his miserable thought. None of this means anything in the greater scheme of things. None of this language belongs in the higher levels of consciousness. She remembered the story of the violinist and the courage he had shown after the awful story of losing his family.

"Sir, you can only live life through your world. Through your filters. If you want to act on the miserable thoughts then that is your choice of course. I chose to acknowledge those thoughts let them pass and then act on the happy ones. The part of me that now shows up is excited about today and my journey. I will also help you with your journey if you let me. Life is for fun and happiness. I will love and help lots of children and lots of adults. I believe we are all connected at a deeper level. We just need to release the stuff we all carry. It doesn't mean anything. Think about it Sir." Ruby held out her hands.

The dark stranger dropped his stick and reached out his hands. In a flash he disappeared.

Ruby continued forward. The turrets of the dark castle were now in full view. Ruby was close to the top.

As she walked proudly towards the entrance of the dark castle, a familiar voice called her name from behind her. Ruby spun round to find her parents standing in the centre of the path.

"Ruby, look at you. It's so sad. You have never been right, we know that. We tried to help you and do our best for you, but you were intent on ruining your life. We feel so sorry for you?" her mother cried. Her father looked frustrated and distant.

Ruby thought it was going too well. A series of emotions hit her hard, sadness, guilt, anger, fear, she suddenly felt wobbly on her feet and grabbed a hanging branch for support.

"What did we ever do to you to deserve this? We have been thinking it over time and time again. You have worried your mother to death Ruby?" her father added.

Ruby knew she was going to have dig deep, she closed her eyes once more and thought about Osclouro's prophecy. My journey is my journey, I know there is good and bad things in life, I have the chance to help people who have suffered worse than me, who have lost all hope. Only through my experience of the world will I be able to demonstrate true empathy, to really understand and to help people through anxiety and depression. There is nothing to be sad, angry, fearful or guilty about. There is just life and I will replace negative emotions with love, compassion and purpose.

"Mum, Dad. I am happy. I have learnt great things in my life and many times I have had to tread a hard path to get those learnings. Many of the great people in history have had difficult lives and then changed the world for the better. I love you that is all you really need to know. You will find your own path to happiness. Do not hold onto any negativity in your worlds. I will always love you" Ruby felt every word. For the first time everything now made complete sense.

Ruby's parents faded away, all that was left was the dark castle in front of her.

As Ruby approached the entrance to the castle, she could see her reflection in the large mirrored doors. There were no handles, so Ruby pushed against the doors, but they were stuck solid.

"So do you like the look of yourself then?" a voice growled at her.

A devil like creature appeared behind her.

"Yes, I do" Ruby replied, surprisingly relaxed.

"So what are you going to do now Ruby?" the creature asked?

"I am going to have fun" Ruby replied.

"You think you are being smart don't you with your clever words, but you have many enemies Ruby. Nobody likes you and your fears will return" The creature grinned.

"Our enemies are just a projection of ourselves, so I will do the best to stay friendly with everybody. I have no expectation of others and I am sure I will have more fears as I walk down more untrodden paths. Don't take life so seriously creature; it really is not worth it" Ruby smiled.

"You may get ill Ruby. You may have an accident and lose a limb. Have you thought about death? You may feel good now, but when you experience these you will fall right back into the dark depths of despair" The creature grinned.

Ruby thought about all the times she had looked to the future and was unable to create a happy thought. This had made her feel worse and the cycle of the fear trap continued. She now understood the illusion, caused by illusionary pressure she had put herself under. It was not real. She thought about the challenges the creature had thrown towards her. In the past every small sensation in her body, every terrifying thought had suggested death. She had been fearful of so much.

Her thinking had now changed. She knew that every time she practiced acceptance, didn't take the game too seriously and enjoyed focusing on her innate purpose then she would float through any challenge. If she lost a limb, then it is still her thinking that would determine her outcome. She would still be life in all its glory, still connected to her innate gifts. Logically she could chose to be happy, or choose to be upset. The external factor of losing a limb or having an illness would still be there in both scenarios. In relation to death, well when it's our time we all pass over to the next stage of the journey, so why bother fearing that? She will stay neutral through good and bad times and will always view life through her new higher level of consciousness.

"I am finding it difficult to connect to your language from this level of consciousness. I feel that you can no longer help me at this particular stage" Ruby smiled gently.

"I will return. You know that don't you Ruby."

"Yes I know. You are the tester. You will help me by challenging if I really mean it?"

"If you have not moved out of your comfort zone, then you haven't lived. If you are not continuingly being tested then you're not living. If you don't crap yourself at least once per day then you are not doing enough" The creature started to move towards Ruby.

The creature emphasised the word "lived" and then continued to mutter on as Ruby stared at herself in the mirror. "You will have nowhere to hide now Ruby, you cannot use anxiety as your excuse anymore. You will miss it you know and then it will come back, because at some level you want it don't you Ruby and when it comes…….."

She was no longer afraid of the tester. She knew it was just a prod to help her move forward. No more judgements of how she was feeling, what was good, what was bad? She was now neutral and happy.

The creature was now right up beside her muttering threats in her ear, Ruby could feel the hot breath of the creature on her cheeks. She stood firm smiling to herself in the mirror, proud of her new relaxed care free attitude.

Suddenly there was an almighty crash, a sound of a musical instrument smashing on the back of the creatures head. The creature immediately retreated and rushed towards to the trees.

Ruby turned around to see a short bearded man smiling with a huge headpiece made out of dried fruit with a violin in his hand. Next to him stood Leon smiling.

"Just about had enough of listening to that claptrap" Fergus said gesturing to the creature to leave.

Ruby rushed forward and hugged Leon and Fergus. Fergus was overwhelmed by the welcome Ruby gave him. It was though they had been friends all their lives.

"I will be back" the creature screamed.

"Yes we know and we look forward to it" Leon laughed.

"I thought you used love and compassion, so how does hitting over the head with a violin fit in?" Ruby challenged light heartily.

"I did it in a loving way. Sometimes a kick up the backside doesn't hurt Ruby" Fergus responded with a cheeky grin.

Fergus turned around and whistled towards the tops of the trees. A huge red dragon swooped down from the sky and landed right beside them.

"I'm so glad to see you Ruby" Ruby kissed the dragon's long nose.

The dragon's tummy rumbled with pleasure.

Leon and Fergus mounted the dragon, "come on Ruby it's time to leave."

Ruby turned back towards the mirrored doorway. "Just wait a second, I will be right there."

"Ruby, if you look in the mirror it will show the future. I advise you to come back. It could be dangerous" Fergus shouted.

Well I have come this far Ruby thought as she positioned herself in front of the mirror.

Fergus shook his head, does anybody ever listen to me?

Ruby felt dreamy as the mirror filled up with a white mist. The mirror was then filled with a splendid colourful wedding scene.

Ruby was excited, it must be my sister's wedding. What a wonderful sunny day it is. The guests were seated either side of the walk leading to the gazebo. Sweet strains of classical music drifted through the crowd.

Balloons and streamers fluttered around the railing and banisters. Ruby recognized her own special displays of flowers a mixture of pink, light blue, and white.

To the left a horse and cart, decked out in ribbons and twisted coils of streamers, stood ready to whisk the groom and bride away. Ruby thought how perfect and lovely everything was. The smell of fresh cut flowers filled the air.

The music stopped, and all heads turned to face the far end of the walk. The opening to the bridal chorus started to play. Ruby could make out the back of the bride as she walked down the aisle, she wore a stunning strapless wedding gown with a two-tier veil and a pearl crystal head-piece. Her father, smiled at the blushing bride as her led her down the aisle.

The music faded, and the groom looked into his brides eyes. Ruby nearly fell backwards with shock. It was not her sister and not Mike her fiancé.

It is Tom and I! She screamed to herself in astonishment.

"Cherished family members and honored guests, I would like to thank you for coming this fine morning," the priest started proceedings.

Ruby could not believe her eyes, this is my future.

After the prayers were over, the priest took them through their vows. An adorable little boy dressed in a light blue tuxedo and a sweet bridesmaid dressed in pink walked up and handed Tom a gold ring.

Who are these children she thought.

"The little girl is Tom's daughter from his first marriage, she will love you dearly Ruby and the cute little boy you adopt together after you get engaged" Leon whispered into Ruby's ear.

"I cannot believe it" Ruby replied.

"What you project out, you get back Ruby, there is always a way to move forward, the light of hope is always there. It's just the way it works. Futures can change, so always hold onto your beliefs and your dreams. You must come now, it is time."

Ruby turned round and gave Leon a huge hug. "Thank you for everything Leon."

"You don't need to thank me Ruby, remember this is just a dream. In reality we are all parts of you. Parts that have been waiting to be unveiled. Take a look" Leon pointed towards the mirror.

Staring back in an orderly row was a friendly group of smiling faces, from left to right. The tester stood with arms crossed giving a mischievous wink. To his right stood the magician waving enthusiastically. Next came Leon and Fergus both displaying assuring grins, followed by the Chief Master from the magicians and doctors' institute tapping his nose. He was the one who sent the secret notes to the magician, Ruby thought. To the side of the Chief Master stood Tala and Luca holding hands. Tala gave an approving punch in the air and Luca blew a kiss. Finally the wizard Osclouro dressed in magenta coloured robes with a friendly smile nodding gracefully.

The collective oneness Ruby thought. They are all part of me. Love, happiness, compassion, wisdom and wellbeing.

"Now you can share this story Ruby and help many more people find peace and happiness. Pure acceptance combined with an exciting journey to the higher levels of consciousness. Those same old things somehow looking and feeling different." Leon put a friendly hand on Ruby's shoulder.

Ruby and Leon put their arms around each other and mounted the dragon. Fergus yelled out in excitement, they were air born in seconds.

In the dark blue sky, full of stars, Ruby could make out the ceiling of her room.

Tomorrow is going to be a great day she thought.

13 THE SECRET TO SUCCESS

1. We all have free will, it's our birth right. We can change our habits.

2. Thoughts are just thoughts. Only act on the ones that raise your levels of consciousness.

3. Accept the feelings and sensations for what they are just sensations.

4. Find a short simple mantra that you can use when you need to dig deep and then distract yourself.

5. Do not fight off the thoughts. Acknowledge them and then let them go, like a train passing in the station.

6. Dance with the sensations; practice reframing them. Do not retreat; do not fight. Put your sword down and face into the things you fear.

7. Relax during activities in the day by practicing the peripheral vision and breathing technique taught by Luca.

8. Find ten minutes each day to meditate, unclench your fists and Ha breathe. Dab water on your forehead and visualise some of beautiful scenes in this story.

9. The more you change your habit, the more things will come automatically. This is the way we are all wired.

10. Keep yourself fit and eat healthy. Avoid excessive alcohol, drugs, heavy smoking or stimulating foods. This will help reduce your arousal trigger level.

11. Avoid blaming the past. Live in the now. Don't bother dwelling on difficult external factors or listening to people who are judging from a lower level of consciousness.

12. Do not measure yourself, just practice. You will soon break out of the fear trap and enjoy life again. Setbacks and tests are just a necessary part of moving forward. Take your foot off the pedal, it will come. It always does.

13. You already have the resources inside you, surrender to this and the veil will lift. The answer lies in getting out of your own way and giving your innate wisdom and wellbeing the space to weave its magic.

14. Always love yourself, no matter what happens. This is your world.

15. What you project out, you get back. It's the way the universe works. So be kind to people and let the expansive, wiser, compassionate you shine. The real you!

16. Rise above situations, and hold onto your innate purpose. It is always loving and compassionate. Set yourself some great and exciting goals for the future and focus your efforts on achieving these.

17. Only take on advice that helps. Question whether it helps you and your purpose. If not, just delete it.

18. Become a master of your emotions and energy. Have fun practicing and playing the game. Don't take life too seriously.

19. Remember, you are not alone. Use your new understanding to help others. We are all in this together.

20. Finally take the pressure of yourself. Your fighting days are over. We are all going through the same journey. Enjoy it, smile, and have fun.

    The end.

ABOUT THE AUTHOR

Nick Chapman's concern over the widespread levels of anxiety witnessed today encouraged him to dedicate many years researching solutions to panic, anxiety, and stress.

Although the triggers differ from individual to individual, many people seem to experience the same common symptoms of fear or worry. Most are reluctant to open up about it or really deal with it because they feel weak or embarrassed. Many are restricting their progress because of their fears, some become unwell. Others follow a very unhealthy lifestyle to compensate for the low times.

Nick travelled the world researching and studying ancient systems, new philosophies and the latest breakthroughs in science, which he incorporates into his work today. Nick's passion for helping clients dissolve anxiety and confidence issues is also born out of his personal journey of overcoming panic disorder.

He now dedicates a large part of his life helping people to overcome their own personal barriers and achieving success in their business and personal lives.

See www.thefeartrap.com